"Here is an ideal combination: Alistair Begg, one of today's stand-out gospel communicators, reflecting on the life, wisdom, and sheer guts of Daniel, one of yesterday's outstanding heroes of the faith. Courage is a common thread that runs through the lives of such men and women. With clarity and grace, it is laid bare before us in these pages as one of our great needs today. *Brave by Faith* is certain to challenge and encourage Christians of every age and at every stage in life. A book for our times!"

SINCLAIR B. FERGUSON, Professor of Systematic Theology, RTS;
Author, *To Seek and to Save* and *Devoted to God*

"Alistair Begg engagingly opens up Daniel 1 – 7 to encourage believers to live an excellent Christian life in the midst of the fiery furnace of national iniquity and injustice. The secret? Trusting and obeying the sovereign God. For, though the world would send God's children to the lions' den, 'the people that do know their God shall be strong, and do exploits' (Daniel 11 v 32). A timely book that is needed today and that can also help us prepare for tomorrow."

JOEL R. BEEKE, President, Puritan Reformed Theological Seminary,
Grand Rapids, Michigan

"*Brave by Faith* could not be more timely. Alistair Begg beautifully paints the ancient biblical story of Daniel, equipping modern readers with enduring truth and courage to live well in grim times. And he gives us a winsome reminder of how our story will actually end."

ELLEN VAUGHN, *New York Times* bestselling author;
Author, *Becoming Elisabeth Elliot*

"With characteristic clarity and warmth, Alistair shows God's people how to make brave choices as a misunderstood minority in challenging times. Like Daniel and his friends, we need a clear understanding that our unchanging, powerful, sovereign God is on the throne and that both the present and the future are in his hands. This book shows how humble, prayerful, calm, obedient trust in our sovereign Lord will shape our choices and our responses as we live in this world as citizens of the eternal kingdom of our Lord Jesus. We can take heart and live bravely because our risen Lord has overcome the world."

JONATHAN PRIME, Associate National Director (Pastoral Ministries) of the Fellowship of Independent Evangelical Churches (FIEC), UK

"Alistair Begg's may be the most recognizable Christian voice on air in America today. In this book, he takes us to the book of Daniel to jolt American and Western Christians awake to the reality of 'exile' in our own land and show how we ought to act in that context. This book is indeed a shock, but though it is blunt, it is also full of hope. Pastor Begg has delivered an elixir: truth and confidence in God. Now is the time for serious people with serious worries to turn to trusted voices that speak bluntly to these times, and that is what Alistair Begg does."

HUGH HEWITT, Radio Talk Show Host; Author; Columnist

"If anything seems to be missing or elusive in the lives of Christians today, it is the presence of courage. One of the virtues of courage is that it holds on to hope. Alistair Begg helps us all by taking us back to the notable Old Testament model for both hope and courage—the prophet Daniel. You will be refreshed and strengthened by a fresh look at the young prophet and his friends as they face life-threatening hostility in a pagan world."

JOHN MACARTHUR, Pastor, Grace Community Church, Sun Valley, California; Chancellor Emeritus, The Master's Seminary

"I have always admired Alistair's God-given courage and conviction in speaking and writing about biblical truth which everyone needs to hear but far too many are afraid to say. In that same spirit, *Brave by Faith* is a phenomenal book with a timely message."

DAVID NASSER, Senior Vice President, Liberty University

"This is a brilliant book. Alistair Begg handles the text beautifully and applies it incisively to the specific challenges we face at this cultural moment. Best of all, reading through Daniel 1 – 7 along with this book refreshed and strengthened my confidence in the Lord Jesus Christ. I can't recommend it highly enough."

GARY MILLAR, Principal, Queensland Theological College, Australia; Author, *Need to Know*

ALISTAIR BEGG

BRAVE

BY FAITH

GOD-SIZED CONFIDENCE IN A

POST-CHRISTIAN WORLD

To Jeff Mills,
a brave and faithful
partner in the gospel

CONTENTS

INTRODUCTION:
THE WIND HAS CHANGED

"These all died in faith ... having acknowledged
that they were strangers and exiles on the earth."
(Hebrews 11 v 13)

"I urge you, as sojourners and exiles..."
(1 Peter 2 v 11)

For many years, I think we've read those verses and thought, "I wonder what it's like to be a stranger, a sojourner, and an exile in this world."

Now we know.

I lived the first 31 years of my life in Scotland. For the last 38, I've lived in the US. And for the first time since I've lived here, I sense a significant shift in the mentality of the people of God. By that I don't mean a change in how people of vague religious spiritual interest are feeling, or even in how church attenders are feeling, but in how those who are committed to serving their Savior Jesus and to obeying his word in the Bible are feeling.

Many of us appear to be completely overwhelmed by the reality that we are no longer a majority and our views are no longer considered acceptable or even expressible.

That's because the wind has changed. If you are reading this in the UK or Australia, you'll know it changed earlier: perhaps a decade or so ago. In the US, it's changed in the past five years. The prevailing wind is no longer at the back of the sails of professing Bible-believing Christians. Indeed, the wind appears to be blowing hard behind the forces of secularism. I'm not an analyst of culture, and I don't want to overstate this; but I don't want to understate it, either. I travel a fair bit around the US, and regularly back to the UK too. And I've seen that the old days of the "Moral Majority" in the US and bravado over all that would be achieved by those endeavors, and the idea of either the UK or the US being a "Christian country," have gone. As Tim Keller describes it:

> *"We are entering a new era in which there is not only no social benefit to being Christian, but an actual social cost. In many places, culture is becoming increasingly hostile toward faith, and beliefs in God, truth, sin, and the afterlife are disappearing in more and more people. Now, culture is producing people for whom Christianity is not only offensive, but incomprehensible."*
> *(https://www.thegospelcoalition.org/article/ how-to-reach-the-west-again/)*

The people of God are now living with the awareness that we are being pushed hard, in the words of the psalmist, and many of us feel we are about to fall (Psalm 118 v 13-14). Secularism and the modern paganism that goes with it are taking their toll.

So I find that American Christians are now looking over the Atlantic Ocean in a way that they hadn't done previously. When Americans I knew used to visit Britain, they would say to me on their return what a wonderful, beautiful, history-soaked place it was to visit; and they would ask me why so many of the churches were so empty. But what is happening now is that American Christians are beginning to realize that our nation is starting to look a lot like Europe. We are starting to feel that the notion of a persecuted church—which we've understood theoretically and who we've prayed for from a distance—is coming ever closer. It's beginning to dawn on us in the West that the things we've sung about may actually be true. Honestly, I had little idea what I was saying when I sang as a child:

> *This world is not my home,*
> *I'm just a-passing through.*
> *My treasures are laid up*
> *Somewhere beyond the blue.*

In reality, for us in the English-speaking West this world has tended to feel very much like home, and our treasures have been right before our eyes. But now we are finally facing the fact that this broken, sinful world in which we live is not actually our home—that what the Bible says concerning believers in this world is really true: that we really are aliens and that we really are strangers. The fact of the matter is that it has always been true that we are strangers in and to this world. It has just been clouded, obscured by the size and influence and legal protection of the church in most of the Western world. But this world is not actually our home. We're not supposed to be settling down here forever. We're not supposed to be treating this life the way other people treat it, as if this is the be-all and end-all of everything, or as if as Christians we can have a comfortable, respectable, prosperous life here and look forward to even more of those things in eternity.

Secularism pushes back again and again against what the Bible says about sexual ethics, about salvation, about education, about the role and reach of the state, or about matters of public welfare. Public opinion has turned against Christians. As the British columnist and social commentator Melanie Phillips puts it, we live in a culture…

> "… which will have no truck with claims such as religious miracles or the existence of God. These are dismissed as the superstitious beliefs of a bygone primitive age of myth and bigotry."
> (The World Turned Upside Down, page 2)

Superstitious bigotry. Suddenly, as a minority group within an increasingly secularized nation, we are finding out how it feels to be outsiders. And we don't like it. We're not used to it. And it's easy to become bewildered, angry, defensive, or defeated.

So the question is, what does it look like to live as a Christian in a society that does not like what Christians believe, what we say, and how we live? How are you going to live in this new normal?

Enter the book of Daniel.

MORE ABOUT BELIEVING THAN BEING

Daniel and his friends had grown up in the promised land, in Judah. As young men, they found themselves being dragged into exile, far away from the society they had known, into a city that neither knew of nor cared about nor was impressed by their faith or their lives. Daniel would live in Babylon from his late teens or early twenties until he was in his eighties or nineties. Most likely he died there. These exiles were understandably fearful of the power that held them in its grip, and were wondering what God was doing and whether they could (or should) keep obeying him in such circumstances.

And so the message of Daniel is incredibly relevant for us in our generation. Not because it maps out a strategy for how to deal with our new lack of status—or to reverse it. Not because Daniel was a great man and we need to follow his example, buck up, and be more like him. Yes, it's a good idea to seek to emulate the men and women of faith we find in the pages of the Bible. But no, this book will not tell you to be like Daniel. Instead, it will call you to believe in Daniel's God. We will be able to navigate our present moment to the extent that we realize that the God of the exiles in the sixth century BC has not changed in the intervening two and a half millennia. As we walk through the twists and turns of the first seven chapters of the book of Daniel, we will see some heroes and some anti-heroes: Daniel, Hananiah, Mishael, and Azariah, and the kings Nebuchadnezzar, Belshazzar, and Darius (and, of course, some lions). But these are not really the heroes of Daniel 1 – 7. Neither are you or I (we weren't even there). God is always the hero of the story. And that is why we need to discover the message of the book of Daniel: to rediscover our confidence in the God who reveals himself there.

This book is therefore going to give you at least six parts God for every one part Daniel or anyone else. For the overarching message is simply this: God is powerful, and God is sovereign, and even in the face of circumstances that appear to be prevailing against his people, we may trust him entirely. The battle may seem to be tilting against the church, but still God reigns supreme. I make no apology for the fact that each chapter's theme is a variation of this message. If the exiles needed a whole book to remind them of and steady them in this great truth, then so do we today.

So how can we, as Christians, keep our courage and hope, in this culture? Is it even worth continuing to live as a Christian? Look to the God whom Daniel knew and we will find out why, and how, to live as his people. We'll see that there is a better way than growing angry, or keeping our heads down, or retreating, or giving up altogether.

Here is how you stand firm and live bravely when the wind is blowing hard against you.

KNOW YOUR LINES

Much is revealed about us in times of crisis.

And the book of Daniel opens with a national and personal crisis. We are in "the third year of the reign of Jehoiakim king of Judah" (Daniel 1 v 1). The people of God—the Jews—are living in the land promised to them by God: Judah. But "Nebuchadnezzar king of Babylon came to Jerusalem and besieged it." Though Babylon, the greatest power in the region, was a huge empire ranged against this tiny kingdom, in one sense there was no need to panic: God's people had been attacked, invaded, and besieged before. They'd looked disaster in the face several times over the years—and each time their God had defended them and brought victory from the jaws of defeat. But that same God had also, through his prophets, warned of what would happen if his people continued to pay no attention to him and continued to pay no more than lip service to obeying his laws in his land.

So then came the catastrophe: "The Lord gave Jehoiakim king of Judah into [Nebuchadnezzar's] hand, with some of the vessels of the house of God" (v 2). The king and a great number of the people were taken into exile in Babylon. The house of God—the temple where he had dwelled among his people—was destroyed. The Babylonian king brought the temple treasures to the land of Shinar, to the house of his god, and placed them there, in the treasury of his god (v 3).

It was the greatest crisis in the history of God's people since Adam and Eve were cast out of Eden. From every viewpoint it looked as though the gods of the Babylonians were stronger than the God of the Bible: the God of Abraham, Isaac, and Jacob. After all, if the God of Abraham, Isaac, and Jacob was strong enough to protect his people, how come the Babylonians were able to come in and give them such a hiding? So the inevitable question must have arisen:

"Where is God in this?"

And we can imagine the Jews forgetting their own disobedience, and the warnings and predictions of the prophets, and asking themselves:

"Did we follow our God for nothing?"

Those must have been the questions in the minds of the parents as their children were rounded up and taken off to Babylon—to "the land of Shinar" (v 2-3). *We didn't raise our children in the faith in order for them to be carried away like this. Our kids need to live in Judah, not in Babylon—what will become of them there? If God is good, why is he causing our children to have to grow up in this kind of place?* After all, those Jewish parents would have known their Scriptures: Babylon, in the land of Shinar, was the place back in Genesis 11 where the Tower of Babel had been constructed. It was the place where mankind had come together to oppose God's purposes for humanity in his world, and had said, *We'll show God who is in charge of this operation: we'll build a tower for ourselves and raise it all the way up to the heavens, and we will decide what to do for ourselves.* This was where the youths of Judah were being taken. How could they survive at all—let alone survive in their faith?

I don't wish to sound alarmist, but the generations that come behind us in the church, perhaps not too far removed from us, may have occasion in our own land to say similar things. Some of us may be asking similar questions because of the circumstances of our own lives or the lives of our children right now: *What is God doing? Why are we having to live in—and why are our kids having to grow up in—this kind of place, this kind of society? If God is good, why would he let our land look like this?*

The book of Daniel is a record of what happened to God's people in the heart of an empire set up to deny and defy God: the story of the exiles told through the particular stories of four men. If and when we feel that our society is heading in a similar direction—that it looks much more like Babylon than Jerusalem, and increasingly so—this is also the story that shows us how we can live with confidence and courage in such a world.

SAYING NO

King Nebuchadnezzar knew how to run an empire. He commanded one of his civil servants to bring the cream of the Jewish crop to his palace so that they could be fashioned—refashioned—in such a way that they would be good Babylonian citizens and servants, and be done with all that old, defeated Israelite worldview.

If we can get our hands on them, the thinking went, *if we can relocate them, educate them, and rename them, then through our brilliant program of subtle and (if necessary) not-so-subtle coercion, we can change the way these fellas think about the world.*

So these young men were taken away from all that was familiar to them—away from security, from routine. A change of location is often enough to change everything about a person; it happens quite routinely today to youngsters who have been professing faith when they go to university. They are no longer going to the same places; they no longer have the constant reinforcement of their family; they no longer attend the church they always have. Just a change of location can be enough for someone to say, *I'll just pause my faith for a while… Maybe I'll give up on it altogether.*

And if that was not enough to overwhelm these young Jews, then a change of education was next. They were going to learn the literature and the language of the Chaldeans—the Babylonians. What you read and how you think changes who you are, and that was the aim with these youngsters. Every powerful state seeks to educate its people—and especially its children—to share its view of the world, its priorities, its definitions of right and wrong and what is acceptable and unacceptable. So did Babylon.

Next, these men were renamed. Daniel, Hananiah, Mishael, and Azariah became Belteshazzar, Shadrach, Meshach, and Abednego—new Babylonian names. They were still god-honoring names, but honoring a different god: the god (or gods) of the Babylonians. Think of how intrinsic to your sense of yourself your name is. These young men were being given a new identity.

And they went along with it. They were relocated, re-educated, and renamed. They had little choice, if they wanted to stay alive.

There was one more aspect to the transforming of these men from Jewish troublemakers to useful, successful Babylonian subjects: "The king assigned them a daily portion of the food that the king ate, and of the wine that he drank" (Daniel 1 v 5).

And they said no.

"Daniel resolved that he would not defile himself with the king's food, or with the wine that he drank" (v 8). They had been unable to prevent themselves being relocated; they could not resist the fact that they were being re-educated; they had been powerless to resist new names being foisted upon them. But they could and they would resist changing their diet.

RESOLVE REVEALED

This seems a strange place to draw a line! But in the Old Testament, one of the distinguishing features of God's people was the rules they followed about what they would and would not eat and drink. Dietary choice for God's people was not just an external manifestation of nothing much; rather, it was an external outworking of their deeply held convictions about what it meant to belong to God. Given where these young men were and what they were doing and what they were being called, the last thread tying them to their Jewish roots and faith was dietary.

So Daniel said, *I can do this, and I can absorb that, but I cannot go any further. I have drawn a line; I will not cross it, and I am taking my stand here.*

Don't mistake Daniel and his friends for rabble-rousers who were a constant nuisance. Don't confuse being godly with being obnoxious. No, Daniel enjoyed "favor and compassion in the sight of the chief of the eunuchs" (v 9). Later on, when they stood before the king, they were by far the wisest and most insightful of their cohort of students, even compared with those who had been born into the Babylonian elites (v 19-20). They were bright, good-looking, and hard-working. They paid attention, showed up on time, and were good students. And yet there was a point they would not go beyond. There was a core to them, and so there was a resolve in them, and that caused them to take this stand and risk the consequences of the king's displeasure (which tended to be fatal).

That kind of resolution doesn't come just as a whim. It doesn't come overnight; it doesn't well up in the moment of challenge. Crisis shows what's inside of a person; it doesn't create it as much as reveal it. And as soon as these men come up against it here, they are ready to say, *No, we are not going to give in.*

Do not let the distance of their time, culture, and geography blind you to the magnitude of their decision. Think of what the exiles must have been tempted to say: *We're a long way from Jerusalem. Things are different now. Times have changed. The prevailing wind is too strong for us to stand against, and resisting it won't make any difference or do any good. We are here in Babylon, and we need to make the best success of life that we can in Babylon. Those things that our fathers insisted upon: they don't really matter that much, do they?* (Don't think that way of thinking is confined to ancient Judean history. It is alive and well in every generation, not least in contemporary evangelicalism.)

Daniel, Hananiah, Mishael, and Azariah refuse to take that approach. A dead fish flows with the current; it takes a live fish to swim against the stream. They are going to swim against the stream. They have drawn their lines, they know where those lines are, and they will not cross them.

PUTTING IT TO THE TEST

Now Daniel needs to persuade the chief of the king's eunuchs to allow them to eat different food. (It's not that if the chief says no, Daniel will give in. It's simply that it's better to get the people in authority to agree to his approach than to have to do it in defiance of them.) The chief likes the four Jews, but he likes his head being on his shoulders more, and he is not willing to risk the king's displeasure in order to let Daniel do what he wants (v 10). *I like you, Daniel,* he says, *and I understand you have your beliefs, but this is not going to fly because I value my life too much. You'll have to fit in on this one, Daniel.*

But Daniel has drawn his line. He doesn't see the chief's response as evidence that God's will is that he and his friends should compromise. He won't give up. The CEO has proven unwilling, so he goes to the COO—the steward—and suggests a deal (v 12-13): *How about you give us ten days of eating only vegetables and water, and then compare our appearance with the appearance of the guys who have been eating the king's food, and "deal with your servants according to what you see?"*

This is gutsy. Daniel is saying, *We're going to put this to the test, we're going to obey what we know to be right, and we're going to trust God to come through for us.*

So the ten days pass, and they all line up, and "it was seen that they were better in appearance and fatter in flesh than all the youths who ate the king's food. So the steward took away their food and the wine they were to drink, and gave them vegetables" (v 15-16)—which they ate for the next three years of training and education. The chief of eunuchs presumably knew nothing of it and must have congratulated himself, as he saw them growing fatter and stronger, that he had refused to let Daniel go without the meat and the wine!

It's worth pointing out as an aside that these verses are not offering us a diet to follow ourselves. After all, Daniel and his friends ended up fatter, not thinner— that was the whole point! And the reason they looked so good at the end of the ten-day test (and after the following three years) was not the Daniel diet; it was the Lord's miracle. This is not about superfoods; it is about the supernatural. God showed himself strong; these men should have looked gaunt and withered and pathetic, but they looked vibrant and terrific and had a glow to their skin. Why? Because God did it. Every day that passed in those three years, when they woke up and looked in the mirror, those four men would have been reminded that God is no man's debtor, and he is able to show himself strong.

HOW TO STAND FIRM

Why were these four men willing and able to know their line, and stand firm and refuse to cross it, when they were being placed under pressure that most of us can only imagine?

Because of what they knew about God.

Three times in this opening chapter, we're told that "God/the Lord gave…" and these words are the key to understanding the chapter.

Verse 2: "the Lord gave Jehoiakim king of Judah into [Nebuchadnezzar's] hand."

Verse 9: "God gave Daniel favor and compassion in the sight of the chief of the eunuchs."

Verse 17: "God gave them learning and skill in all literature and wisdom."

God is in control. He is in control of great geopolitical events; the Babylonian invasion and victory happened because God gave Nebuchadnezzar that victory. The God who had given them great blessing through Judah's history and their lives was also the God who had given the besiegers victory. God was responsible for the exile of his people; God was responsible for the destruction of his temple. Nebuchadnezzar would take the credit, but the Lord was the one who oversaw it.

And God is in control of interpersonal interactions and individual outcomes. Imagine the end of the three years of training when the king commanded that all the students, including our four guys, should be brought before him. Imagine the chief of the eunuchs bringing them in, confident now because of their appearance and their progress: *Here they are, your majesty. The program has worked exceptionally well. They're exceptional. Just look at them, and then just ask them. You can see they are fine with their new names. They are well-versed in our literature and philosophy. In terms of physical fitness, these four are stand-outs. This internship program is a clear success.*

But what the king and his chief didn't know was that God—the God of Abraham, Isaac, and Jacob—was in control. God was in control of Daniel, Hananiah, Mishael, and Azariah's relocation, God oversaw their re-education, and God granted them resolve and grace as they took their stand. God took them into Babylon; God was with them in Babylon; and (as we'll see) God would use them in Babylon.

ANOTHER LINE

As Daniel stands before the chief of eunuchs and tells him that he has resolved that he will not defile himself with the king's food or with his wine, no matter what, we can see echoes of another man, living in a far more hostile foreign land, standing before a far more powerful enemy, and drawing his lines and refusing to move. After all, even if we can begin to wrap our heads round the sheer otherness of Babylon for the Jewish exiles, we are still nowhere near understanding the foreignness of this earth to the Lord Jesus when he left the glory of heaven and stepped down into the limitations of time and space and the difficulties of this broken world. He was willing to become one of us, to live in a world that was bent on resisting his Father. But he was not willing to disobey, even after forty days alone in the wilderness:

> *"And he ate nothing during those days. And when they were ended, he was hungry. The devil said to him, 'If you are the Son of God, command this stone to become bread.' And Jesus answered him, 'It is written, "Man shall not live by bread alone."'"*
> *(Luke 4 v 2-4)*

KNOW YOUR GOD

So the real emphasis of this chapter, as with every chapter of Daniel, is not so much Daniel as God. You and I will only live brave like Daniel did if we first know the God who Daniel did. Here is the God Daniel knew from a young age. Back in Judah, when Daniel was growing up with his family, with no inkling of the Babylonian crisis that was to come, he would have recited this at the beginning and end of the day:

> *"Hear, O Israel: The LORD our God, the LORD is one. You shall love the LORD your God with all your heart and with all your soul and with all your might." (Deuteronomy 6 v 4-5)*

And though years later Daniel found himself in an alien environment with a different name, reading different books, and hearing a different language, with his land invaded, his king defeated, and his temple eviscerated, he was not going to stop loving the God who he knew, and who he knew stood behind all things, including the worst things.

Here is the God who has given us every situation and every challenge we find ourselves in, and who is in control of our country and our century as much as he was over Babylon in the sixth century BC. We are not, and never have been, in Israel. We do not in fact live in a "city on the hill," for no nation today enjoys a special status before God. Where is Jerusalem today? It is not in the US; it is not in the UK (despite William Blake's hopes that it could be built in England's green and pleasant land); it is not in the Middle East, either. It is in heaven. Our Lord Jesus told the Roman governor Pilate that his kingdom was not of this world (John 18 v 36). No—we live in this world, in "Babylon." But God's kingdom, and not my nation, is where we belong and where we will be at home, and if we confuse the two, we open ourselves up to confused loyalties and a compromised faith.

We are in Babylon—and God is sovereign even here. Nothing is actually out of control and nothing is about to get out of control. But, given the push-back of twenty-first century secularism, you and I are going to face challenges. The crises will come; the moments will arrive when we are called to go with the flow of our culture rather than obedience to our God in the workplace, or the sports club, or in how we raise our children, or what we say from our pulpits, and so on. Those crises will reveal what is inside us. Don't assume you'll stand firm in those moments. Equally, don't assume you will have to give in. Resolve now. Think through where to draw the lines you will not cross.

We will not necessarily all draw all our lines in the same places. Take the promotion of the transgender agenda in public (state-run) schools. One Christian teacher will resign before having anything to do with it. Another may stay and seek to teach Christian ethics to those who otherwise may not hear that there is a different view, resigning only if forced herself to promote transgenderism. One may be willing to wear a rainbow lanyard with his ID badge; another not. One set of Christian parents will not send their children to public school at all; another will do so, but ensure that they are positively teaching God's design for men and women in the home and give themselves financial margin to homeschool their kids if necessary. The lines may be drawn in different places, but drawn they should be, and crossed they must not be.

That is just one terrain on which lines have to be carefully, thoughtfully, prayerfully drawn. There are many others. So, know your lines. And know the God who will give you all you need in the situation he has put you into, to enable you to stand firm for him and say, *No, I am not going to give in.*

KEEP YOUR CONFIDENCE

King Nebuchadnezzar was powerful and successful—the leader of the most mighty nation on the face of the known earth. If people in his day had seen him, they would have been awestruck by his splendor, his power, and his significance. Think about the power and the prestige of the office of the President of the United States and you're about halfway to glimpsing Nebuchadnezzar's exalted status in his empire and throughout the world.

He was hardly human. But in one crucial way he was very, very human.

He had a recurring nightmare.

THE DREAMS OF A KING

In his dream, Nebuchadnezzar saw a great statue of a man, and "its appearance was frightening. The head of this image was of fine gold, its chest and arms of silver, its middle and thighs of bronze, its legs of iron, its feet partly of iron and partly of clay" (Daniel 2 v 31-33).

Then, as the king watched his dream develop…

> *"a stone was cut out by no human hand, and it
> struck the image on its feet of iron and clay, and
> broke them in pieces. Then the iron, the clay, the
> bronze, the silver, and the gold, all together were
> broken in pieces, and became like the chaff of the
> summer threshing floors; and the wind carried
> them away, so that not a trace of them could be
> found. But the stone that struck the image became
> a great mountain and filled the whole earth."*
>
> *(v 34-35)*

Nebuchadnezzar does not enjoy his nighttime vision: "His spirit was troubled, and his sleep left him" (v 1). Concerns that look merely problematic in the daylight become paralyzing in the darkness of the night, and there are things that we can handle or hold at bay when we're vertical that overwhelm us when we are horizontal. As the Phantom puts it in the musical *The Phantom of the Opera*, "Nighttime sharpens, heightens each sensation; darkness wakes and stirs imagination." Nebuchadnezzar may be the mightiest of rulers, but he is reduced to a trembling insomniac by this dream.

So he does what kings did at that time—he calls for his wise men: the magicians, the enchanters, the sorcerers, the Chaldean elite (v 2). He has a very straightforward request: *Tell me the dream and its interpretation.* Being a king who is used to getting his own way, he uses the carrot-and-stick motivational technique: *If you don't tell me what I dreamed and what it means, I will have you torn limb from limb and pull your houses down. On the other hand, if you do tell me, you will receive honor and reward beyond anyone's dreams.*

But these wise men can't answer. They don't know what the dream was, so they can't make up some interpretation of it that will please the king. "The thing the king asks is difficult, and no one can show it to the king except the gods, whose dwelling is not with flesh" (v 11).

It's a good point! But the king is too desperate and too used to getting his own way (and perhaps too exhausted) to listen to logic; he "was angry and very furious, and commanded that all the wise men of Babylon be destroyed. So the decree went out, and the wise men were about to be killed" (v 12-13).

Here we see what happens when insecurity, anger, and power combine. It's an amazing response—to condemn to death all his advisers because they cannot do something that is impossible. But it is not an unusual form of behavior, nor only an ancient one. The twentieth-century theologian Reinhold Niebuhr, in his book *The Nature and Destiny of Man*, suggests that modern political tyranny may be traced to a darkly conscious realization of the insecurity of man's existence; the excesses and atrocities of people in power may speak to the fact that, in their deepest hearts, they're not really in control of anything at all. We can still see that insecurity manifested on the world stage today.

This reaches into our homes and hearts too, doesn't it? However large or small our own empire, aren't our angry outbursts and our irrational responses when things don't fall out the way we would like signs that we know deep down that we are not in control, and that we do not like that truth? Or, to put it a different way, we know deep down that we are not God, and we do not like that truth. As the 19th-century philosopher Friedrich Nietzsche once said, "If there were gods, how could I bear not to be a god?"

Nebuchadnezzar is used to being the master of his destiny, the captain of his ship—so we ought not to be surprised that this king, who believes himself to be so powerful and so significant, is rendered so insecure by this nightmare and is prompted to such atrocity by his lack of control over events.

And it's at this point that Daniel and his friends find themselves in the firing line—because, having graduated from the University of Babylon in chapter 1, they are now numbered among the king's advisers, and so they're on the death list.

GOLD, SILVER, BRONZE, IRON – AND THE STONE THAT BREAKS THEM ALL

We'll return to Daniel's response to the threat to his life later in this chapter, but in his own "vision of the night" the God of heaven gives him knowledge of and insight into the meaning of the king's dream (Daniel 2 v 19). So Daniel heads straight to Arioch, "whom the king had appointed to destroy the wise men of Babylon" and says, "Do not destroy the wise men of Babylon; bring me in before the king, and I will show the king the interpretation" (v 24).

Here is what it means: "You, O king, the king of kings ... you are the head of gold" (v 37-38). *This is a good start,* you can imagine Nebuchadnezzar thinking. *I don't know why I worried about it so much and got so furious with everyone about it. I shouldn't have threatened to ex-ecute you, Daniel: you're a good man.* He starts sitting up a little higher in his throne... but then Daniel goes on.

> *"Another kingdom inferior to you shall arise after you, and yet a third kingdom ... and there shall be a fourth kingdom..." (v 39-40)*

That's what the silver, bronze, and iron represent. The four empires have traditionally been identified (accurately, I think) as Babylon, Medo-Persia, Greece, and Rome. To go further than that is speculation, which is rarely helpful (not that that has prevented countless books being written and sermons preached about what each toe equals, and so on). Rather than engaging in speculation, it's best to restrict ourselves to the point of Daniel's God-given interpretation: to stand back from the painting, as it were, so we can see the whole thing and the effect the divine artist is wishing to bring through. What is the big story shown by this painting? It is this: that God sets up and God brings down kingdoms; so these kingdoms, however mighty and however brutal, will come and go. And then...

> *"... the God of heaven will set up a kingdom that shall never be destroyed, nor shall the kingdom be left to another people. It shall break in pieces all these kingdoms, and bring them to an end, and it shall stand forever, just as [the king] saw that a stone was cut from a mountain by no human hand, and that it broke in pieces the iron, the bronze, the clay, the silver, and the gold." (v 44-45)*

You can imagine the king tensing up and slumping down on his throne somewhat. But perhaps this Judean upstart is mistaken? It is, after all, only one interpretation, right?

> *"A great God has made known to the king what shall be after this. The dream is certain, and its interpretation sure." (v 45)*

Here is the main and the plain thing: human history is under the control of God, and he has a purpose which will be achieved. The message of the dream was for the young exile as much as for the apparently all-powerful king. God would replace every kingdom and bring into being his everlasting kingdom.

And so it was that the Babylonian kingdom was overrun by the Medo-Persians. The Medo-Persian Empire was taken over by Greece when it was defeated in battle by Alexander the Great. Alexander the Great's empire divided, and soon enough the Roman Empire took over. And the Roman Empire ruled most of the known world (except my home country of Scotland—I'd like to think it was because of our courageous refusal to bow the knee, but it's more likely the Romans just weren't interested in it). Roman power smashed armies, obliterated nations, toppled kings, and imposed its culture everywhere its legions led. But at pretty much the highpoint of Roman rule, in a backwater province of the Middle East, a teenage virgin had an angelic visitor who announced to her that she would have a son and that his name would be Jesus, "and the Lord God will give to him the throne of his father David [the greatest inhabitant of Judah, the greatest of Israel's kings], and he will reign over the house of Jacob forever, and of his kingdom there will be no end" (Luke 1 v 32-33).

"How will this be," this girl famously answered, "since I am a virgin?"

God will do it, the angel in essence answered. *He will take care of it. Your son will be the one who will one day announce that because he has arrived, "the kingdom of God is at hand" (Mark 1 v 15).*

Jesus was (and still is) the stone that God fashioned out of nowhere. Here was the everlasting kingdom of God. Many of his countrymen pinned their hopes on him. Here, surely, was the king who would overthrow the Romans. Here was the one who would rule in Jerusalem and restore God's people to freedom and power. And then all those hopes and dreams came to a crashing halt because the king was nailed up on a Roman cross. The statue had smashed the stone. But it was not possible for death to keep hold of this king (Acts 2 v 24). And he then told his subjects to go out into all the world in the power of his Spirit and call people of all nations to enter his kingdom through bowing their knee to him and accepting him as their Lord and Savior, until the day when he would return to rule visibly and universally over his world-encompassing kingdom.

And though at the turn of the first century it must have seemed impossible that the Roman Empire would ever fade and perish, fade and perish it did, even as the kingdom of King Jesus grew throughout the Roman Empire and beyond its borders. The stone smashed the statue, and the stone became a mountain that filled the entire earth. It is an international kingdom. It is a people, a language, a tribe, and a tongue that comprehensibly, universally covers the entire globe. Its size and breadth make Babylon look limited, and the magnificence of its king shows Nebuchadnezzar up for what he always was: a mere man.

This was the message of the dream for the exile and the king, and for us: God is God, God is in control, and God's kingdom has no rivals.

NO NEED TO PANIC

What does this mean for us? Daniel's reaction, first when he heard of the death sentence and then when God revealed the king's dream to him, should be instructive for us. There's no panic. He doesn't try to run for the borders, nor does he sit around waiting for the inevitable steel on his neck.

No: he gathers with his fellow believers and he prays: "Daniel went to his house and made the matter known to Hananiah, Mishael, and Azariah, his companions, and told them to seek mercy from the God of heaven concerning this mystery, so that Daniel and his companions might not be destroyed" (Daniel 2 v 17-18). Daniel does not want to die. So he asks for mercy from the God who, he knows, can help.

And then once he has received the interpretation from God, he praises God for who he is:

> *"Blessed be the name of God forever and ever,*
> *to whom belong wisdom and might.*
> *He changes times and seasons;*
> *he removes kings and sets up kings;*
> *he gives wisdom to the wise*
> *and knowledge to those who have understanding;*

he reveals deep and hidden things;
  he knows what is in the darkness,
  and the light dwells with him.
To you, O God of my fathers,
  I give thanks and praise,
for you have given me wisdom and might,
  and have now made known to me what we asked
of you,
  for you have made known to us the king's
matter." (v 20-23)

Notice the difference between what Daniel is saying here and what the enchanters had said in verse 11: "The thing that the king asks is difficult, and no one can show it to the king except the gods, whose dwelling is not with flesh." In other words, they were responding in terms of the polytheistic worldview of the Babylonian culture. In the Babylonian religion, there were all kinds of gods for all kinds of things. That was a given. Daniel responds very differently, not only with a confidence that sees him actually speak to the God in whom he believes but with a very clear statement that there is one God—one God who changes the seasons, sets up and brings down rulers, and reveals what he wills to whom he will.

Contemporary Western nations are, in this sense, not very different than ancient Babylon. Our friends increasingly are filled with talk of the gods, if we have ears to listen: the god of work, the god of sexual expression, the god of power, the god of golf, the god of weather, and so on. To paraphrase the twentieth-century writer G.K. Chesterton, when people cease to believe in the God of

Daniel's fathers—the God who has revealed himself in Scripture—they do not believe in nothing; no, they believe in just about anything. And the only God whom the culture will not, cannot, put up with is this God who says and shows that he is the one true God. So this is where the Christian parts company with the culture, for when the modern Western mind thinks of religions, the word that immediately springs forward is the word "tolerance." But, as John Stott pointed out, people do not "always stop to define what they mean by it":

> "It may help if we distinguish between three kinds [of tolerance]. The first may be called legal tolerance, which ensures that every minority's religious and political rights ... are adequately protected in law. This is obviously right ... Another kind is social tolerance, which encourages respect for all persons, whatever views they may hold, and seeks to understand and appreciate their position. This too is a virtue which Christians wish to cultivate ...
>
> "But what about intellectual tolerance, which is the third kind? To cultivate a mind so broad that it can tolerate every opinion, without ever detecting anything in it to reject, is not a virtue; it is the vice of the feeble-minded. It can degenerate into an unprincipled confusion of truth with error and goodness with evil. Christians, who believe that truth and goodness have been revealed in Christ, cannot possibly come to terms with it."
>
> *(Authentic Christianity, page 69)*

The opposite is also true: today's Western societies, in which the majority of people believe that truth and goodness are relative and to be intuited by individuals for themselves, cannot possibly come to terms with the gospel message. Our society does not mind if we want to include our little god somewhere in the pantheon of contemporary gods, but if we insist that the God of the Bible is the God of the universe, and there is no other beside him, then we meet a very different reaction.

That should not make us panic. Nor should it make us rude; Daniel replied to the man sent to kill him "with prudence and discretion" (v 14), and you will search in vain through the whole book that bears his name for one of God's people responding aggressively, angrily or condescendingly to any pagan. We know that there is a God who has revealed himself in his Son, and who, through that Son, has brought about the kingdom that cannot be extinguished or overthrown. That should make us confident, even as it should make us prepared to find that our view is considered intolerable.

DON'T HANG UP YOUR HARPS

This is why we refuse to hang up our harps. In Psalm 137, we meet some of the exiles, and here is what they do and how they feel:

> *"By the rivers of Babylon we sat and wept*
> *when we remembered Zion*
> *There on the poplars*
> *we hung our harps,*
> *for there our captors asked us for songs,*

> *our tormentors demanded songs of joy;*
> *they said, 'Sing us one of the songs of Zion!'*
> *How can we sing the songs of the LORD*
> *while in a foreign land?" (v 1-4, NIV)*

They looked back at the good old days, and they wept. Then they hung their harps up, for there seemed to be nothing to sing about in Babylon as they faced the taunts of their tormentors. But I don't think Daniel and his companions were there as they did so. Of course it was right to weep over what had been lost, and the sin that had seen it lost—but it was no less right to be working hard, serving well, staying faithful, praying hard. Why? Because God's people could know that there would always be something to sing about because Babylon would not win and Babylon would not endure, for a stone would smash it and grow into a mountain.

We have seen more evidence of God's grace and goodness than Daniel did. We have seen the stone arrive; we know the name of the king whom death could not hold; we can look back in history and around in our world and see how the stone became a mountain. Yet some of us have just hung up our harps. We find ourselves complaining about everything, looking back to the good old days and worrying that the church cannot survive the empire of aggressive secular post-Christendom. Too much of the public face of evangelicalism is characterized by vociferous, angry venting or panicking, rather than prayerful, humble, calm, and confident belief in a sovereign God who is in control of things.

How will we handle the onset of persecution? How

will we handle the loss of our jobs on account of our Christian faith? How will we handle the closing down of public worship? Will we hang up our harps, believing that all the good things are in the rearview mirror? Not if we remember that God is God, that God is in control, and that God's kingdom ultimately knows no rivals.

In the 1920s, Lord Reith helped to establish the BBC—the British Broadcasting Corporation—and then from 1927 served as its first Director-General. He was a somewhat severe man from the highlands of Scotland. As the BBC began to be carried along by the tide of secularism that swept through Britain in the sixties, a young producer stood up in a meeting and said to Lord Reith that the world was changing, and that the BBC did not need to continue with its religious programming output. People were no longer interested in it, he said, and the church was becoming increasingly obsolete.

Lord Reith, who was 6'6" tall, stood up, told this young man to take his seat, and said:

"The church will stand at the grave of the BBC."

And you know what? It will. It will still stand when the BBC, and CNN and Fox as well, dwindle and die. The kingdom of God will stand when every organization and institution and empire meets its end. "Do not be afraid, little flock, for it is your Father's good pleasure to give you the kingdom" (Luke 12 v 32).

Your church may seem small. As you drive to meet with the household of God on a Sunday, you may pass hundreds of houses whose inhabitants give not a thought to what you are doing, except politely (or not so politely) to deride it. It may feel little. But the kingdom of God is unsmashable, and it has an embassy in your neighborhood that we call the local church. Don't be discouraged as you meet; don't be distraught over dwindling numbers or a more and more hostile media. Instead, commit to it. Serve your church family. Give yourself to it. Because, when the Lord builds his church (either in number or in maturity) through our labors, gifts, and giving, we are being used to build the only kingdom that will last forever. There is nothing coming next. So, give your best to this kingdom. It may feel small, but it is never in vain, for this kingdom is eternal, and it is God's.

God is sovereign over the affairs of time, including those times when everything seems to have gone completely pear-shaped. That is the lesson of Daniel 2. God sets up and God brings down kingdoms. These kingdoms will come and go, but God has established a kingdom that will never come to an end and will never be passed on to somebody else. That, says Daniel, is what we need to know. So we do not panic and we do not vent, and we enjoy a deep confidence even as the tides seem to run against our faith, for God is God, he is in control, and his kingdom—his church—ultimately knows no rivals.

So we leave Daniel and his friends doing better than ever. Their heads are still on their shoulders; and they are moved up the ranks of Nebuchadnezzar's civil service (v 48-49). Babylon is treating them well. They have remained faithful, and they have enjoyed promotion. But it will not last...

OBEY GOD (DESPITE THE CONSEQUENCES)

When it is all on the line, who will you worship? When the moment of choice comes, who will you obey?

That moment arrives in stark form for Daniel's three friends in the third chapter of the book of Daniel. And that moment arrives for us, too, in one way or another. The consequences of obeying God were stark for them, and they will be increasingly stark for us, too, in our "post-Christian" culture. For there are plenty of gods that society demands you bow to, and none of them are the God of the Bible.

ALL THE PEOPLES WORSHIPED

Around nine years have passed since Nebuchadnezzar responded to Daniel's interpretation of his dream by saying, "Truly your God is God of gods and Lord of kings, and a revealer of mysteries, for you have been able to reveal this mystery" (2 v 47). What happens now on the plain of Dura—also known as Shinar—shows that though the king had been charmed by the revelation of his dream, he had not been changed by it. He sounded very positive about Daniel's God—but it was superficial. As the seventeenth-century commentator Matthew Henry put it, "Strong convictions often come short of sound conversions." In those nine years, the king's memory of the meaning of the dream seems to have dissipated, other than the description of him as the gold head. So now he makes a golden image 90 feet high, and sets it up, and he gathers his most powerful men from all over his empire and has his herald proclaim:

> *"You are commanded, O peoples, nations and languages, that when you hear the sound of the horn, pipe, lyre, trigon, harp, bagpipe, and every kind of music, you are to fall down and worship the golden image that King Nebuchadnezzar has set up." (3 v 4-5)*

Nebuchadnezzar hasn't just forgotten his dream; he's forgotten his history. He's setting up his image on the same plain where his ancestors set up their tower. Throughout the Bible we see Babylon and Jerusalem set against one other: Babylon representing man and his proud defiance against God and determination to construct a society without God; and Jerusalem representing God and his revelation, and the submission of people to his law and to his rule. Nebuchadnezzar is taking his stand with Babylon, and this image is essentially a symbol of the power of Babylon and the greatness of its king. He, like the builders of the Tower of Babel, wants to ensure his name is great.

To make sure that everyone does as he wants and worships his image, he informs them that "whoever does not fall down and worship shall immediately be cast into a burning fiery furnace" (v 6). This was no idle threat: the prophet Jeremiah had reminded God's people only a few decades before of "Zedekiah and Ahab [probably two false prophets in Judah], whom the king of Babylon roasted in the fire" (Jeremiah 29 v 21). This is no funny little joke; this is literally deadly serious. Nebuchadnezzar is saying, *I have had this amazing image put up, and I want submission and worship from everyone, or else.* And, unsurprisingly, everyone says, *Ok—we will bow.* Perhaps for most of them the sight of this magnificent image was sufficient to cause them to bow. Perhaps for some of them, the sight of everyone else bowing made it clear that it was the right thing to do. And for the rest of them, the thought of the furnace was more than enough to get their knees to bend: "As soon as all the peoples heard the sound of the horn, pipe, lyre, trigon, harp, bagpipe, and every kind of music, all the peoples, nations, and languages fell down and worshiped the golden image that King Nebuchadnezzar had set up" (Daniel 3 v 7).

ALL OF US STILL WORSHIP

What is going on here? It's simple: idolatry—worshiping something that a human has made instead of worshiping the God who made humans. The people who gathered on that plain were bowing to an image as though it were God. Whether it was because they were impressed by what they saw or because they wanted to fit in with everyone else, or because of the threat of what would happen if they did not, they chose to bow to the image, and so they made it an idol.

Idolatry is not only a problem of ancient civilizations. It is a problem of all human societies because it is a problem of human hearts. Romans 1 is speaking of everyone when it says that...

> *"although they knew God [deep down], they did not*
> *honor him as God or give thanks to him ...*
> *Claiming to be wise, they became fools, and*
> *exchanged the glory of the immortal God for*
> *images resembling mortal man ... [they] worshiped*
> *and served the creature rather than the Creator."*
> *(Romans 1 v 21-23, 25)*

As a result of that idolatry, "God gave them up in the lusts of their hearts to impurity, to the dishonoring of their bodies among themselves" (Romans 1 v 24). Idolatry—in your life and more broadly in society—precedes immorality. If we would understand why immorality is tolerated or even promoted, we need to look behind the behavior to the worship—to the idol.

Of course, the idols change; few people in the West bow down to golden images today. But the idols have no less a hold, and our reasons for bowing to them are no different—they look impressive, our peers are worshiping them, and our society threatens us with penalties if we do not join in. As Paul Simon put it in *The Sound of Silence*, "The people bowed and prayed / To the neon god they made."

Great swaths of humanity bow down at various shrines—temples, malls, offices, strip bars—with great sincerity of heart, and every one of them represents a false religion.

It is far easier to identify the idols in other cultures than in our own. There are idols we bow down to not because we're made to but because we want to, and those are the very hardest to acknowledge. To take two examples: first, the average Western Christian parent finds it natural to worship the idol of children, at the expense of fidelity to God and service of his people. Of course kids are a good thing—idols usually are—but they so easily and unnoticeably become a god. It becomes so vitally important that Tommy goes swimming and Zadie has skating and Rochelle does her tutoring, and maybe they won't have time to go to the church youth group, and maybe we won't have time as a family to read the Bible together each day. The word of God and the people of God are important, but the greatest commitment is to the kids. When push comes to shove, we worship the image of the perfect family, and the holy God can fit in around that.

Second, the average American Christian finds it natural to worship the idol of politics. We think and pray and speak as though if our guy wins, the kingdom wins; and if he loses, then it's hell. In other words, we treat our favorite for President, or our political party, as a god. American Christians are used to having a political home, and we have forgotten that this is Babylon—it may be Republican Babylon or Democrat Babylon, right-wing Babylon or left-wing Babylon, but it is Babylon nonetheless—and we have forgotten that the kingdom of God is not of this world. My sense is that in the US most of us worship

capitalism, and none of us have any idea of what socialism actually is. Neither builds the kingdom of God; as
the economist John Kenneth Galbraith once memorably
put it, "Under capitalism, man exploits man; while under
socialism just the reverse is true."

But set up a political party or economic system as an
idol and you'll make sacrifices to it. Witness the ethical backflips that Christians on both sides of the divide
(sadly, it's more of a chasm) have started to perform to
defend the biblically indefensible. There is no nuance
and no ability to see the strengths and weaknesses of
either our own position or the positions taken by others.
It's idolatry—confidence in something other than God
to deliver what we need. So we bow down to the idol of
party, and we attend our chosen network temples of Fox
News or CNN and MSNBC. We don't think—we just
rearrange our prejudices. One way to discover if you are
bowing down is to ask yourself this: do you watch, and
seriously consider, the views of the networks that embrace
the other view to yours? If not, then when push comes
to shove we are worshiping the image of President and
party, and the holy God can fit in around that.

The list could go on: status, acquisition, our bodies...
These are the things that our culture worships, and so
these are the gods to which we bow without thinking.
Our hearts naturally worship idols that exalt our agenda,
our goals, our significance, or our reputation. Christian
faith does not mean that we are immune to idolatry; but
it does mean that we have no excuse not to dismantle our
idols. A Christian is not someone who does not struggle
with idol-worship, but they are someone who prays:

The dearest idol I have known,
Whate'er that idol be,
Help me to tear it from its throne
And worship only thee.

But they weren't praying that on the plain of Dura. The agenda, goals, significance, and reputation of those men gathered there were best furthered and protected by worshiping Nebuchadnezzar's image. So they all did.

All except three.

WE WILL NOT

Some of the Chaldeans—who were presumably jealous that Daniel's friends Shadrach, Meshach, and Abednego had been promoted over their heads—noticed that the knees of these three men remained unbowed when the music started up. So they went and (having helpfully reminded Nebuchadnezzar about the threat of the fiery furnace) told the king:

> *"These men, O king, pay no attention to you: they*
> *do not serve your gods or worship the golden image*
> *that you have set up." (Daniel 3 v 12)*

The king, furious, summons the three Jews. *Is it true?* he asks them. And then he spells out the consequences for them:

> *"If you are ready … to fall down and worship the*
> *image that I have made, well and good. But if you*
> *do not worship, you shall immediately be cast into*

> *a burning fiery furnace. And who is the god who*
> *will deliver you out of my hands?" (v 15)*

Sometimes as I read a Bible story, I wish I didn't already know how it turns out. This is one of them. Imagine reading without knowing how it plays out. What would these three men say? What would they choose? What would happen? You would be biting your fingernails at this point. These men are facing the furnace—being burned alive. How will they answer?

What would you have said? *Would you have bowed down?*

Think about it. It is only a one-off deal. What's the problem with just once? And you'd know the statue is just a joke; it's not God and doesn't have power. Why not bow down? You're far from home; no one would know. No one is asking you to actually renounce God. You don't have to say anything. Everyone else is doing it, and no one will notice you joining in. And the king has, after all, been very good to you—you owe him your job, your house. Yes, your conscience is nagging at you, but it will quieten down after a bit. Plus, if you bow down, you won't die, and if you don't die, then you can be useful to God. And God wants us to be useful to him, so that's a good argument for just bowing down, real fast, getting it done and getting on with living. Plus, that furnace is hot.

Here is what Daniel's friends decide to answer:

> *"O Nebuchadnezzar, we have no need to answer*
> *you in this matter. If this be so, our God whom we*
> *serve is able to deliver us from the burning fiery*

furnace, and he will deliver us out of your hand,
O king. But if not, be it known to you, O king,
that we will not serve your gods or worship the
golden image that you have set up." (v 16-18)

This is remarkable. They are saying, *Our God is able to*
rescue us. We don't assume that he will, but to answer your
question, O king, there is a God who can deliver us. And even
if he doesn't, we are not going to worship this golden idol you
have set up.

Why did they say this? Because they believed that what
God said in his law he actually meant:

> *"You shall not make for yourself a carved image, or*
> *any likeness of anything that is in heaven above,*
> *or that is in the earth beneath, or that is in the*
> *water under the earth. You shall not bow down to*
> *them or serve them, for I the LORD your God am a*
> *jealous God." (Exodus 20 v 4-5)*

For them, that was the beginning and the end of it. They
were not going to do it because God told them not to do
it. *We're going to obey him,* they said, *and if that means we*
die in a furnace, then we die in a furnace. And if it means
that God intervenes dramatically, then we won't die in the
furnace. But our part is to obey him. We will not bow to your
image, king.

Don't miss this. They don't know that they'll be res-
cued. They know God could do it—but they are not as-
suming that he will. *And still they obey.* This is faith. As
a friend of mine once said to me, "Faith is not believing

in spite of evidence; rather, it is obeying in spite of the consequences." Cynics often tell us that, as Christians, we believe even though there's no evidence. Well, dealing with that is for another book. But more challenging to us as believers is the truth that Christian faith shows itself in obedience despite the consequences. Faith says what these three men said to the king. It says what Martin Luther told the emperor when he was called to renounce the truths of the Bible or face being burned at the stake:

"Here I stand. I can do no other. God help me. Amen."

DISCIPLESHIP IS OBEDIENCE

What we are talking about here is simply discipleship. I have no doubt that Peter, when he wrote to first-century Christians facing persecution, had Daniel 3 in mind when he said:

"Beloved, do not be surprised at the fiery trial when it comes upon you to test you, as though something strange were happening to you." (1 Peter 4 v 12)

Facing the fire as we live obedient to God and refuse to worship what our society bows down to is not strange; it is the normal life of the believer—in Daniel's day, in Peter's, and in ours. Faith is still obedience despite the consequences.

We are called to obey even when it won't work out well for us. We are called to obey even when it seems better not to. Pragmatism is the enemy of obedience. When we base our decision-making on what looks more sensible or beneficial or understandable, then, when it comes to it, we're going to worship our culture's idols instead of obeying God. When we base the Christian life on doing what is most suitable, amenable, or comfortable, we are extracting it from what the Bible says discipleship actually looks like. The Christian life is sometimes going to look like resisting the attractiveness of an idol, refusing to meet the expectations of everyone else, and accepting the consequences of mockery, ostracization, unemployment, and worse. We are not called to be pragmatic but faithful: to say, *God has said this, and so I will do it.* What will see us hold the line is a simple, straightforward, unerring obedience to the word of God—even if that means the fiery furnace.

THE GOD WHO DELIVERS

Babylonian furnaces at that time were used for the firing of bricks (the kind of bricks that the builders at Babel would have used to build their proud, God-defying tower); the fuel was charcoal and the furnaces produced temperatures as high as 1,800 degrees fahrenheit (1,000 degrees centigrade). They looked a bit like railway tunnels, blocked at one end and with an entrance at the other. And the now-furious Nebuchadnezzar made sure that the furnace into which Meshach, Shadrach, and Abednego would be thrown was seven times hotter than normal (Daniel 3 v 19). It was so hot that the soldiers whom he ordered to throw in the three men were themselves burned to death (v 22).

So what happened next is a miracle:

> *"King Nebuchadnezzar was astonished and rose up in haste. He declared to his counselors, 'Did we not cast three men bound into the fire?' They answered and said to the king, 'True, O king.' He answered and said, 'But I see four men unbound, walking in the midst of the fire, and they are not hurt; and the appearance of the fourth is like a son of the gods.'*
>
> *"Then Nebuchadnezzar came near to the door of the burning fiery furnace; he declared, 'Shadrach, Meshach, and Abednego, servants of the Most High God, come out, and come here!' Then Shadrach, Meshach, and Abednego came out from the fire. And the satraps, the prefects, the governors, and the king's counselors gathered together and saw that the fire had not had any power over the bodies of those men. The hair of their heads was not singed, their cloaks were not harmed, and no smell of fire had come upon them." (v 24-27)*

A lot of ink has been spilled about, and a lot of arguments prompted by, the identity of the fourth person. I'm inclined to think of him as an angel, though many see him as a manifestation of the pre-incarnate Jesus. Either way, Nebuchadnezzar's question has been answered. "Who is the god who will deliver you out of my hands?" he asked (v 15), the inference being that there is no god powerful enough to thwart the king of Babylon. Now he has his answer. Who is the god who can deliver? This one.

Our God is the God who delivers. He delivered his people from the bondage of Egypt, bringing them out with his outstretched hand. He delivered his people from the power of the Philistines, through the victory of his king, David. He would deliver his people from the exile that he had delivered them into, through changing the heart of another, later, king: Cyrus of Persia. And supremely, he delivered his people from our bondage to sin and death and judgment through the death and resurrection of his Son, our Lord Jesus.

So we have a deliverance to look back to that surpasses even the one that Shadrach, Meshach, and Abednego could remember after they had come through the furnace. Yes, they had been delivered by one who looked like the son of the gods, who had joined with them in the fire; but they would die again. We have been delivered by the Son of God, who went into the fire of the hell of God's judgment for us, and who gave his life to deliver us, forever, so that whoever believes in him shall never ultimately die (John 11 v 25-26). The most terrifying furnace you and I could ever face—the furnace that each of us should face—has already been walked through by the Lord Jesus, on the cross.

THROUGH THE FURNACE

That furnace of judgment and hell is one we will never face. God has delivered us from it. But notice that when it comes to the "fiery trials" of the Christian life, we are delivered through the furnace, not from it. Obedience to Jesus does not mean we skip the fires; indeed, often obedience will bring us into the fires. It is in the midst of the fire that God often shows himself the most clearly to us and reveals his strength to us:

When through fiery trials, thy pathway shall lie,
His grace all sufficient shall be thy supply.
For he will be with thee in trouble to bless
And sanctify to thee thy deepest distress.

I have known little of trials, so I am not greatly qualified to talk much about trials and suffering. But I have found that the most progress I've made in my Christian life has not come through success and laughter but through disappointment and difficulty and tears.

I learned this early in my Christian life, and I am grateful that I did. When I was a young man at seminary, my mother died of a massive heart attack. My sisters were 11 and 15. Suddenly, my theology had to move from theory to practice, for an open grave had reached into the very core of my existence. And I discovered that as I walked forward through that time, clinging to the Lord in faith and obedience, his grace proved all-sufficient, and he used my deepest distress to mold and shape me. I have watched others, in far deeper trials, testify to the same truth: that it is in trials that the Christian is formed, and in trials that we find the greatest blessings. So when we shun trials, we miss blessings.

I WILL NOT BOW

This is what discipleship takes. We are to offer our bodies (and our careers, our prospects, our respect among our peers, our houses, our bank balances) as living sacrifices to God, holy and acceptable to the Lord. This is the way we worship (Romans 12 v 1). It should be said of you and me what the king ends up saying of Shadrach, Meshach, and Abednego:

> *"[They] trusted in [their God], and set aside the king's command, and yielded up their bodies rather than serve and worship any god except their own God." (Daniel 3 v 28)*

That requires us to reject me-first idolatry. It calls us to be clear-sighted enough to see the idols our culture is worshiping, and the idols our own hearts are drawn toward, because we understand that if we cannot name them, it is not that there are no idols for us to contend with but that we are worshiping them without realizing. It means that we know how to complete the sentences "I will not bow to…" and "I will not bow when…" (Perhaps pause right now to consider how you would complete those sentences.) And it means that we will sometimes say to those around us, *I will not bow.* It demands that we reject a pragmatic, safety-first approach to our Christian lives. It looks like obedience in spite of the consequences. And we will only live this way to the extent that we learn to say, *God has already delivered me from the most fiery of furnaces. He is able to deliver me from whatever you may do to me and whatever I may lose. But even if he does not, know that I will not worship these idols.*

SPEAK OUT (BECAUSE
GOD IS BIG)

The extent to which we truly believe in the God of Daniel will be demonstrated by the confidence of our evangelism in a pagan culture.

In the West there is no doubt that, in many ways, talking to non-Christians—be they neighbors and colleagues or presidents and kings—is harder than it was a generation ago, even than a few years ago. The West's Christian heritage is draining away; those we speak with are often either apathetic about or antagonistic toward the gospel message. Talk about Jesus and you risk being met not with interest or politeness but with hostility and rejection.

And so, many of us don't.

And, not speaking about Jesus, we notice that no one around us is coming to faith—and so we conclude that no one ever will. Our silence becomes a self-fulfilling prophecy.

What is the answer? It is to remember what our part is in evangelism, and what God's part is.

Think of the most hardened atheist you know. Think of the person whose lifestyle is lived in clearest rejection of the gospel. Think of the person who, if you are honest, you simply cannot conceive of bending the knee to Jesus as Lord.

What would it take for them to come to faith?

It will take God's humbling work and a godly person's courageous words—just as it did for King Nebuchadnezzar, perhaps the most unlikely convert in all of history and certainly the most unlikely convert in the Babylonian Empire.

THE WORK OF GOD

Nebuchadnezzar himself recounts how God worked in his life. His story starts out with him enjoying being "at ease in my house and prospering in my palace" (Daniel 4 v 3) when, once more, his dreams begin to haunt him. While he's at ease and while he's prospering, into his life comes this unexpected intrusion that he cannot ignore, in just the same way that one can come to any one of us with a single call from the doctor's office about some blood tests.

Again his magicians and enchanters fail dismally to tell him what it means. (These characters are reliably, consistently, magnificently incompetent, and you would think he would have learned not to bother asking them by this stage.) Daniel, though, is once again able to discern the meaning of the dream, and he warns the king, "It is a decree of the Most High ... that you shall be driven from among men, and your dwelling shall be with the beasts of the field ... till you know that the

Most High rules the kingdom of men and gives it to whom he will" (v 24-25). It is a message of judgment and destruction.

Daniel therefore tells the king that he needs to take action: "O king, let my counsel be acceptable to you: break off your sins by practicing righteousness, and your iniquities by showing mercy to the oppressed, that there may perhaps be a lengthening of your prosperity." *Be sufficiently humble to repent, though you are the king,* Daniel says, *and God may mercifully grant that you will not face this judgment on your pride.*

But the king does not follow Daniel's counsel:

> *"All this came upon King Nebuchadnezzar. At the end of twelve months he was walking on the roof of the royal palace of Babylon, and the king answered and said, 'Is not this great Babylon, which I have built by my mighty power as a royal residence and for the glory of my majesty?' While the words were still in the king's mouth, there fell a voice from heaven, 'O King Nebuchadnezzar, to you it is spoken: The kingdom has departed from you, and you shall be driven from among men, and your dwelling shall be with the beasts of the field. And you shall be made to eat grass like an ox, and seven periods of time shall pass over you, until you know that the Most High rules the kingdom of men and gives it to whom he will.' Immediately the word was fulfilled against Nebuchadnezzar. He was driven from among men and ate grass like an ox, and his body was*

wet with the dew of heaven till his hair grew as long as eagles' feathers, and his nails were like birds' claws." (v 28-33)

Why did "all this [come] upon King Nebuchadnezzar" (v 28)? Because he ignored the message and resisted the opportunity. God in his mercy gave him twelve months before the reality fell upon him. God is slow to chide and he is swift to bless. As Paul put it, God's patient kindness is intended to lead people to repentance (Romans 2 v 4). But pride that is not repented of does come before a fall. It was at that moment of proud triumph that Nebuchadnezzar heard the dreadful words: his kingdom was no longer his own, and nor was his sanity. God brought him down low when his heart was most lifted up.

But why was God doing this? In order that he might truly lift him up. John Calvin, commenting on the way in which God works in the life of a person not unlike Nebuchadnezzar, wrote, "When God, therefore, wishes to lead us to repentance, he is compelled to repeat his blows continually." The blows were painful but the purpose was glorious—to bring a man to repentance and salvation.

That was what God was doing in Nebuchadnezzar's life here. The king had a great deal of pride, so he required a great number of lowering blows. Why would God bother? Not because Nebuchadnezzar was majestic but because God is merciful. God was showing King Nebuchadnezzar that in truth he was not a mighty, self-sufficient, all-powerful ruler but a lowly, needy, dependent creature.

It was only from his lowered, humbled, awful position that Nebuchadnezzar finally...

> "... *lifted my eyes to heaven, and my reason returned to me, and I blessed the Most High, and praised and honored him who lives forever, for his dominion is an everlasting dominion, and his kingdom endures from generation to generation; all the inhabitants of the earth are accounted as nothing, and he does according to his will among the host of heaven and among the inhabitants of the earth; and none can stay his hand or say to him, 'What have you done?'"* (Daniel 4 v 34-35)

God took away, and God gave back. Nebuchadnezzar got his kingdom back, but not his pride. *God is infinitely bigger than me,* the king is saying. *He is greater—he is the ultimate ruler, and next to him I am nothing.* His pride gives way to praise.

You can imagine the counselors and lords in Babylon seeing the king restored to his mind and his throne and saying, *It's good to have the old Nebuchadnezzar back again,* and Nebuchadnezzar answering, *No. I'm not at all the same. I now understand that God is bigger than me, and he is sovereign, not me. Listen: look at me and see that "those who walk in pride he is able to humble."*

God had worked to humble this great king and then to lift him up, utterly changed. So Nebuchadnezzar began looking back over what God had done to and for him, by calling everyone to listen to him so that he could tell them, "It has seemed good to me to show..."

How do you think the average Babylonian citizen would have expected that sentence to finish? It has seemed good to me...

... to show my architectural achievements

... to show my hanging gardens

... to show how successful I've been militarily

No: "it has seemed good to me to show the signs and wonders that the Most High God has done for me" (v 2). His signs. His wonders. When you have been humbled and raised up by the sovereign God, you speak more of him than you do of yourself.

What does it take for a man such as Nebuchadnezzar to come to faith? It takes the work of God in his life. And part of the way God worked was through the words of Daniel.

COMPASSION SPEAKS

Let us rewind to Daniel's entrance into the scene, after Nebuchadnezzar had his dream. When called upon by Nebuchadnezzar—this man who had hauled him from his home, had almost had him killed in a paranoid rage, and had then thrown his friends into a fiery furnace— Daniel realized that the king's dream was a promise of coming judgment on the king. And then something remarkable happened:

> *"Then Daniel, whose name was Belteshazzar, was dismayed for a while, and his thoughts alarmed him ... [he] answered [the king] and said, 'My lord, may the dream be for those who hate you and its interpretation for your enemies!'" (v 19)*

Daniel is not glad that the king is facing this horrendous, God-wrought humiliation. There is no desire for retribution: *Well, king, you put me here, you tried to kill my friends, and now you are really going to get it.* Quite the opposite— Daniel says, *I'm going to tell you what is going to happen, but I want you to know that I wish it wasn't for you. I wish that you weren't facing this.*

Judgment is coming, but Daniel does not exult in that; rather, he has compassion for the one who is facing it. And that compassion drives Daniel to speak: to warn the king of what will happen if he does not "break off your sins by practicing righteousness, and your iniquities by showing mercy to the oppressed" (v 27), and to call the king to "know that the Most High rules the kingdom of men and gives it to whom he will" (v 25).

In his compassion, Daniel does not speak comfort to King Nebuchadnezzar. No, out of compassion he speaks truth to power, and he appeals to him to repent before his humiliation. Daniel is not vindictive, nor is he quiet. He calls the king to repent of his pride and to bow before God while the dream is still a dream and not yet a reality.

Daniel had a sufficient fear of God's judgment that he did not wish it even on his enemy. And he had a sufficient confidence in God's power and mercy that he called this great king to repent.

Daniel could have kept quiet. He was in a foreign land, speaking to a hostile king. Instead, he spoke truth with compassion and conviction. Why? Because he knew God's role in evangelism, and he knew his own.

And so must we.

MY JOB AND GOD'S JOB

My friend Rico Tice, in his book *Honest Evangelism*, points out how we often feel when we seek to share the gospel with our friends:

> *"The problem with actually doing evangelism is that it just doesn't work. You're never successful—people don't become Christians. The other problem is that you might get it wrong. You're not good enough at it … If you feel like that, you're right. Your evangelism will never make someone come to faith in Christ. And your evangelism will never be good enough to win someone. But here's the thing; it doesn't have to be. That's not your job. When it comes to witnessing, the most liberating truth is to realise what our job is, and what God's job is." (page 62)*

So what *is* our job? It is this: to faithfully proclaim the gospel. And what is God's? It is to sovereignly, mercifully work through what his servants say. That is what we see in Daniel 4, and it is what we see throughout Scripture. Perhaps clearest of all is the apostle Paul's experience in the Greek city of Philippi when, on his first Sabbath there, he went "outside the city gate to the river, where [he] expected to find a place of prayer" and "sat down and began to speak to the women who had gathered there" (Acts 16 v 13, NIV). One of those women was a successful businesswoman named Lydia, and…

> *"the Lord opened her heart to respond to Paul's message." (v 14, NIV)*

Paul's role was to give her the gospel message. The Lord's role was to bring her to the place where she would meet a Christian who would share the gospel with her, and then to open her heart so that she received it with repentance and faith. John Stott says of this verse:

> "Although the message was Paul's, the saving initiative was God's. Paul's preaching was not effective in itself; the Lord worked through it."
> (The Message of Acts, page 263)

Whether it be a king or a businesswoman, God can and does bring someone to a place where they can hear the gospel, and he can and does work in their hearts to enable them to receive the gospel and respond in repentance and faith. And so, as Rico points out:

> "Think of the person you know who seems least likely ever to come to Christ in faith. Then think of the power that created light for the first time. Do you think God can't bring them to faith? Do you think the Spirit cannot work to recreate their hearts? The Spirit's power should give us the confidence to cross the office or the street or the front room and tell someone about Jesus ... it is my job, and your job, to tell someone about Jesus—who he is, why he came and what [that] means [for them]. It is not our job to make someone respond. It's God who opens blind eyes. You communicate the message—and then you pray that he would do the miracle." (Honest Evangelism, pages 63-64)

If I asked you to think of someone you know who is unlikely ever to come to Christ, whose name springs to mind? For a while in my life, my answer would have been one particular man I knew back in Scotland who, for the purposes of this book, we'll call Andrew.

A BOOK, A FUNERAL, AND A BAPTISM

Andrew was a physicist who worked not far from the church I pastored. His wife started bringing her three girls to a group for kids that we ran—and so it was that I went to visit her home and met Andrew for the first time.

He was polite. But he was also very dismissive of Christianity—he made it clear that he thought that it was nice for his wife and his girls but it was not and never would be his thing. He was one of those men who seemed a very unlikely convert.

But I dropped a short book introducing the Christian faith through his door, and to my surprise he started coming to church with his family. Still, he would not look at me as I preached, and nothing seemed to be going in. His wife fell pregnant again, and they had a son, who we'll call George. George was born with a life-threatening congenital heart disorder. The whole church was praying for the family, and that little George would live long enough for surgery successfully to be performed, and that his father would be so thankful to God for his work in his son that he'd bow down and worship him.

George died.

I did the funeral. I carried that little boy's tiny coffin to the graveside.

Andrew was now surely the least likely convert in Scotland—a man who had never shown much of an interest in the gospel, a scientist who did not think he needed God, and now a grieving father of a child whose life had been prayed for by a church but who had nevertheless died.

To my surprise, Andrew continued to come to church. And one day, after a sermon on Psalm 23 v 3, which I felt afterwards was one of the worst attempts to explain that verse in the history of Christendom, he came to me and said, "I get it." (This was a shock—I hadn't really "got" the verse myself, and I was the preacher.) "I need the righteousness that only God can give." And so it was that, not many months after we buried his baby son, we baptized this man.

And so it is that, years later, when I doubt that God can bring someone to faith, I remember that physicist back in Scotland. And I remember that my role is simply this: to speak gospel truth where and when I can, with compassion and conviction—and then to pray that God would be at work to open that person's heart. He is the one, and the only one, who is able to do the miracle and give someone faith in the gospel message that they have heard.

IS YOUR GOD TOO SMALL?

It's seventy years now since J.B. Phillips wrote a book which quickly became something of a Christian classic: *Your God Is Too Small*.

In his book, Phillips essentially explores inadequate concepts of God that he says are present among the people of God in a way that is not only an insult to God but has a negative impact on their ability to follow and serve God. Then he goes on to show the greatness of God as he reveals himself in Scripture.

I think that in many places in the West in the seven decades since Phillips first published that book, God has become smaller in his church's estimation as well as in the culture's. We doubt his power. We doubt his control. We doubt his ability to grow his kingdom by bringing people to faith. We grow angry or fearful, as though the forces of modern secularism might overcome the Creator God or cause the end of his church. And we grow silent in our evangelism.

So, let us restore our vision of God as he really is. He is the God who was able to humble the king of Babylon, and then to raise him up to praise him and worship him. Daniel knew that, and so he spoke truth to the king with compassion and conviction. He is the God who was able to open the heart of a businesswoman on the banks of a river outside Philippi so that she placed her faith in his Son. Paul knew that, and so he spoke to Lydia about the gospel. He is the God who in our day is still able to work in the lives of those around us, preparing them to hear the gospel and preparing them to respond to it.

Is your God big enough? If you remember that this is who God is and what he can do, you will pray for those around you, and you will share the gospel with them. You will risk their apathy or antagonism, just as Daniel did, in order to ensure that they hear the truth from your lips. There can be no pleasure on our part in knowing that those who oppose the gospel, mock our God, and malign us as his people are facing the final, unending judgment of God. And there should be no soft-pedaling on our part in warning of that judgment—we must not turn our gospel message into one of how super people are, and how God can offer one or two upgrades to their innate awesomeness. No—we must be clear that the gospel tells us how dreadful we really are, and how in need of God's mercy we are, and how undeserved yet unfailing that mercy is. The gospel is not, *I was a little anxious and I needed peace* or, *I was a little lost and needed some direction in my life* or, *I was somewhat poor financially and needed some cash.* No—it is, *I was blind but now I see.* It is, *I was facing judgment and in my pride I could not see it, but God humbled me, showed me my need, and gave me his mercy.*

When that is our message, as it was Daniel's, God is big enough to use our words and his direct work in order to bring anyone—anyone—to repentance and faith. Even kings, presidents, and prime ministers. Even the most aggressively atheist colleague you have, or the neighbor God has placed you near who is most antagonistic or indifferent to the gospel.

Your job, and mine, is not to convert people. It is to communicate the gospel. God is big enough to do the rest, according to his sovereign plan to build his church.

SEE THROUGH THE GLITTER

5

All it takes is for God to lift a finger, and everything changes.

Between Daniel 4 and 5, there is probably a gap of about 30 years—and a lot of forgetting. Nebuchadnezzar has died, and the ruler now sitting on his throne is a man named Belshazzar. He was the son of Nabonidus and ruled, it seems, in a kind of co-regency position with his father, who had seized the throne from Nebuchadnezzar's infant grandson. (In 5 v 2, where Nebuchadnezzar is described as Belshazzar's "father," it means in the sense of "hugely significant predecessor.")

And as chapter 5 opens, Belshazzar feels popular, secure, and successful—so much so that he holds a huge party to celebrate how great he is.

As is de rigueur for such events, the wine was flowing fast (v 1-2). We're meant to understand that this was an event of great opulence, of extravagance, of a lack of sobriety, certainly of a lack of decency, and—crucially—an event unfolding with no regard for the Most High God.

Belshazzar was showing off his prominence, and in the course of doing so, as the wine began to take hold, he "commanded that the vessels of gold and of silver that Nebuchadnezzar his father had taken out of the temple in Jerusalem be brought, that the king and his lords, his wives, and his concubines might drink from them" (v 2). And that was exactly what they did. It was 50 years or so since these items had been stolen from the temple of the living God and brought into the ownership of the Babylonian kings. And now this Babylonian king took the arrogance and godlessness up a notch and used the vessels made to worship the Creator God to get drunk and to praise "the gods of gold and silver, bronze, iron, wood, and stone" (v 4).

So this banquet is an amazing expression of pride and of sacrilege and of idolatry. Belshazzar is leading his people in saying, *Hey, this is what we think of your God. He's nothing anymore. We're using the symbols of his power and his presence to enjoy ourselves and toast our gods.* Just imagine being one of the thousand invited guests at this event. Everybody would have looked up at the top table and said, *Oh, to be Belshazzar. What an amazing man he is—so powerful, so magnificent, so vastly wealthy. Such a great and impressive ruler.* Here is a man who knows he is a success, laughing at God and using God's gifts to declare his rebellion against and autonomy from his Creator.

But all it takes is for the God he is mocking to lift a finger, and everything changes.

GOD LIFTS HIS FINGER

As Belshazzar raises the cup taken from God's temple and uses it to proclaim his greatness (and drunkenness) and the superiority of his made-up gods...

> *"immediately the fingers of a human hand appeared and wrote on the plaster of the wall of the king's palace, opposite the lampstand. And the king saw the hand as it wrote. Then the king's color changed, and his thoughts alarmed him; his limbs gave way, and his knees knocked together." (v 5-6)*

It's an amazing moment. Here is this man, Belshazzar, who stands in front of this select thousand, apparently in control of the whole world. We would say he's on top of the world. And it only takes the movement of God's finger to completely change the scene.

Much happens between the words appearing on the wall and their explanation—and we shall return to the intervening verses later. But verse 25 reveals the content of the writing the king sees on the wall. The three words themselves are simply three different weights that were used to weigh precious metals on a scale. But they carry a terrifying message for Belshazzar:

Mene, mene: God has numbered the days of the king's rule—indeed, of his very kingdom.

Tekel: Belshazzar has been weighed and found wanting.

Peres: His kingdom has already been given to the Medes and Persians.

And then come perhaps the most chilling words of the chapter: *"That very night..."* (v 30). That very night, while Belshazzar was showing off his power, was vaunting the security of his exalted position, and was proving that he could afford to mock God rather than worship him… that very night "Belshazzar the Chaldean king was killed. And Darius the Mede received the kingdom."

All the time Belshazzar was enjoying his party, Medo-Persian soldiers were working their way into his citadel. The ancient Persian historian Xenophon records how Darius' soldiers dammed up a portion of the Euphrates River, part of which ran under the walls of Babylon, in such a way that they created a marshy area that made it possible for them to walk through the river without being up to their necks. They directed it into a marshland, making it possible for their soldiers to wade through the shallow water, down the riverbed, under the wall, into the city and into the palace. There, they killed the king. While Belshazzar was proudly proclaiming that he was in charge of everything, his walls were being breached. "That very night…"

Belshazzar means *O Bel* (Bel being Marduk, the main deity of Babylon), *protect the king*. What an irony. Even as he was declaring his autonomy, his judgment had begun.

THE WORLD IS HAVING A PARTY

As we see Belshazzar and his friends celebrating, a mirror is held up to our own society. Our culture works very hard to celebrate its success; to pronounce its autonomy from its Creator God; to declare that it has no need of the God of the Bible and his ways anymore. Most of the time, the affluent West is having a party, and using all the gifts God has showered upon us to ignore him or mock his commands. All over our cities, people still arrange parties and hold events (COVID-19 restrictions notwithstanding) to proclaim their greatness and showcase their achievements, not realizing that there is a God who made them and who gives them their gifts and indeed their breath.

But in our day, as in Belshazzar's, judgment has already begun. Belshazzar is a single vivid exemplification of the general rule of humanity that Paul lays out in Romans 1:

> *"The wrath of God is revealed from heaven against all ungodliness and unrighteousness of men, who by their unrighteousness suppress the truth. For what can be known about God is plain to them, because God has shown it to them. For his invisible attributes, namely, his eternal power and divine nature, have been clearly perceived, ever since the creation of the world, in the things that have been made. So they are without excuse. For although they knew God, they did not honor him as God or give thanks to him..." (Romans 1 v 18-21)*

By instinct, we all suppress the truth of what we know to be true about God. We can see it all around us, if we would open our eyes. If we are ignorant of God, it is because we choose to be so. It's not that Belshazzar started drinking wine at his party that night and so his view of reality became skewed. No, his view of reality was skewed, and so he staged his party and drank his wine.

What can be known about God is plain to all people everywhere, because God has shown it to them. His invisible qualities—his power and his divinity—can be seen simply by looking at creation. In other words, atheism is a choice; it is a rebellion against God. The fool has closed their eyes to the truth, has said in their heart that there is no God, and has built out their beliefs and their life from there.

So this age is in a sense no different to any other since Genesis 3, or to this scene at the opening of Daniel 5. We take what God has given and then announce that we don't like God or his ways, so we will not believe in him. We'd rather have a God who agrees with us and with how we want to behave: a God who is accessible and malleable; a God who we can keep or change as we wish; a God who answers to us rather than us answering to him. That is a very contemporary perspective, and yet it is also a very Daniel-5 perspective. We've just changed the names of the gods.

And God says to all people today what he said to Belshazzar through Daniel back then: *Don't ever come to me and say you didn't know. You cannot claim ignorance. Look at creation, at my works there. Look back through history at my works in the past, even in your own heritage and perhaps family. You know all this, and yet you still choose to shake your fist at me.*

So judgment has begun. Though our culture scoffs at the notion (just as Belshazzar would have, as he lifted the cup from the temple to his lips), it remains true that "the coming of the Lord is at hand ... behold, the Judge is standing at the door" (James 5 v 8, 9). Jesus is coming, at the door of this world just as the Persians were at the gates of Belshazzar's city. The writing is on the wall, or rather on the tomb: God "commands all people everywhere to repent, because he has fixed a day on which he will judge the world in righteousness by a man whom he has appointed; and of this he has given assurance to all by raising him from the dead" (Acts 17 v 30-31). In the resurrection of Jesus, God has declared that this world will face his just judgment for its declaration of autonomy from its Maker. We do not know the date; but he does, and it is marked in the divine diary. All it takes is for him to lift his finger and the door will open and that day will have arrived. It will come as a surprise to our society—but no one will be able to say that they have not been warned. The evidence of creation and the evidence of the empty tomb are more than sufficient.

And if we remember this, it will change the way we live while the world declares its success and celebrates its autonomy from the God whom we worship. For there was one old man who was not invited to Belshazzar's party, and it is to his part in these events that we turn now.

FROM THE SIDELINES TO CENTER STAGE

Daniel had risen to become one of the foremost men in Babylon under Nebuchadnezzar. But Belshazzar has no idea who he even is. When his mother mentions this now-elderly Jew, she does not use his name: "There is a man in your kingdom in whom is the spirit of the holy gods. In the days of your father, light and understanding and wisdom like the wisdom of the gods were found in him" (Daniel 5 v 11). And even though Belshazzar's mother remembers Daniel, she has forgotten his God and views him through the lens of a pagan worldview.

Daniel's God has fallen very much out of fashion among the Babylonian elite; and Daniel himself has been completely sidelined by the new regime, and his name means nothing to its king.

But now Belshazzar, his own wise men having proven themselves once again unable to give any actual wisdom, has nowhere else to turn—and so Daniel is fetched and brought in. We're not told where he was or what he was doing, but he must have been in his eighties by this stage. Maybe he was walking his dog or sitting in a rocking chair. And they came and found him: *Hey, Daniel. You still doing that riddle stuff? We know you haven't done it for a while, but surely you still have it in you?* they say. *What's the problem?* asks this elderly man of God. *Well, Belshazzar's completely freaked out up at the palace. There's some handwriting on the wall. His mother's telling him to get you to come up there. Will you come up?*

And so there takes place a conversation between this confused king and the elderly man of God. What is remarkable is that even at this point, Belshazzar is still so proud. He does not describe Daniel as a wise man or thank him for coming. He describes him as "that Daniel, one of the exiles of Judah, whom the king my father brought from Judah" (v 13). He's trying to show that he's still the one in charge—it's a power play to put Daniel in his place. *Tell me what I want to know,* he adds, *and I shall give you wealth and power.* John Calvin says that he treats him as though he were interviewing a prisoner. He meets the one man who has an answer to his questions, and he treats him with sneering pride.

Daniel is unimpressed: "Let your gifts be for yourself,

and give your rewards to another" (v 17). *You can keep the outfit. You can keep your stuff. I don't need your gold chains.* He sees through the gold and the glitter. He sees divine reality rather than the superficial majesty standing before him. He is wonderfully unimpressed by what this powerful and impressive ruler (in the world's eyes) is offering him. Why? Because he knows what the writing on the wall means. He knows that Belshazzar, for all his popularity, status, and wealth, is facing judgment that very night. He knows that God has lifted his finger, and so Belshazzar has nothing he can offer that Daniel needs. He knows that by the end of the night, only one of them will be alive, and it won't be the king.

So Daniel explains reality to the king. He reminds him of what happened to Nebuchadnezzar, and how his ancestor's heart...

> "... *was lifted up and his spirit was hardened, so that he dealt proudly [and so] he was brought down from his kingly throne, and his glory was taken from him ... until he knew that the Most High God rules the kingdom of mankind and sets it over whom he will.*" (v 20, 21)

Then he comes to the point: "You his son, Belshazzar, have not humbled your heart, though you knew all this, but you have lifted up yourself against the Lord of heaven" (v 22-23). *Think about what you've done tonight, Belshazzar,* he says. *You have been guilty of pride, you've been guilty of sacrilege, you've been guilty of idolatry, and you have chosen not to honor God.*

This is the pivotal point. Belshazzar has chosen not to humble his heart but to vaunt his pride.

Pride is at the very heart of human rejection of God. We do not want to accept that there is someone other than us who is in charge of our lives and who gives us our breath and our every success. Pride is at the very heart of it, from the fall of Satan to eating the fruit in the Garden of Eden and beyond, down through history to Belshazzar and on into our own day. Every pastoral collapse that I have observed in my decades of ministry can in the end be traced to one thing: pride—a lack of humility and a vaunting of power or prestige or security or success.

And on the surface, it can look so impressive. Pride draws a crowd, pride projects greatness, pride moves you up in the world's estimation. But all it takes is for God to lift a finger, and everything changes.

And that is what has happened to this Babylonian king.

WE DO NOT NEED THE REWARDS

So here is what the church today can learn from Belshazzar's treatment of and conversation with Daniel. We should not be surprised that there are times when God's people are sidelined by a society which is sure that the church's God is irrelevant and which does not want to hear the church's opinion or insight. There will be times when the gospel is so little thought about that its very nature is forgotten. And the likelihood is that those times are coming to us as the West enters a phase (and like all phases, it will not last) of "post-Christendom." In many ways, it is already here.

One area where we particularly see this is in that of sexual ethics. Melanie Phillips gives the example, all the way back in 2009 (and the train has continued on apace since then), of the beauty queen Carrie Prejean. Prejean was deprived of the Miss USA title because she answered a question from a judge in the contest about same-sex marriage by saying that while it was good that Americans could vote for the rules they wanted, she thought marriage should be between a man and a woman (*The World Turned Upside Down*, page 102). And, Phillips points out:

> *"In Britain the antidiscrimination orthodoxy [of our age] has led to a systematic campaign against Christians—particularly over the issue of homosexuality, the key area where Christians run up against social libertarianism in the public square ... While true prejudice against homosexuals or anyone else is reprehensible, 'prejudice' has been redefined to include the expression of normative values ... in the cause of nonjudgmentalism, only those who are in favor of moral judgments based on the ethical codes of the Bible are to be judged and condemned." (page 101)*

Daniel knew what it was like to be sidelined, and worse. Who knows for how many years Daniel was unwelcome at the palace, unheard in the counsel of advisors to the king, forgotten about and ignored by those at the heart of the culture and government? He and his beliefs had not changed since the days of Nebuchadnezzar, and he had not forgotten what God had shown him during the days of Nebuchadnezzar; but Babylon had changed, and Babylon had forgotten. What did Daniel do? He remained faithful, and he did not change in order to be acceptable. The winds of change did not move him. And neither must they move God's servants today. Faithfulness may lead us to be sidelined and then be remembered only to be mocked; but when the price tag for access to those in power is compromising on the gospel, it is a price too high to pay.

Equally, in times of crisis we should not be surprised to be welcomed back and offered the world. Perhaps that will be the time of greatest danger; for the temptation to accept the trinkets of the world will be great after a season in the wilderness, and the temptation to "soften" the gospel in order for it to be acceptable to our world will be great after a season of being ignored.

Imagine a Christian worker who, after years of being passed over for promotion and mocked behind her back (and sometimes to her face) because she refuses to bend her Christian principles in the workplace, is suddenly summoned to see her CEO. He offers her promotion and a hugely enhanced compensation package, and asks for her opinion of and approval for a new direction for the company because she is known for being a person of integrity. The temptation for her to fall into line will be great.

Imagine a pastor who, after years of service without being noticed by anyone in power, is suddenly invited to the Governor's residence to give advice on some policy or another and offered a place on an advisory council. The temptation to rubberstamp a policy without challenging years of sinful decision-making will be huge.

What must the believer remember in these kinds of situations, when the world suddenly changes its scowl to a smile? That the world can give nothing to us that we may keep. That the world is facing the judgment of the God we know as our Lord and Savior. That what the world most needs from the church is our gospel, not our approval. "Let your gifts be for yourself, and give your rewards to another."

The resurrection of Jesus Christ from the dead lies in history. That is God's assurance to the world that "he has fixed a day on which he will judge the world." The writing is on the wall. Western culture may party in celebration of its success and autonomy—but this is the last night of the party, and the morning will come as the Lord lifts his finger and judgment arrives. And better then to have been sidelined and mocked than to have compromised and joined the party.

6
SERVE WELL,
STAND FIRM

The story of Daniel and the lions' den is the most familiar in the book of Daniel and one of the most famous in all the Bible. Even people who have never read the Bible will know that Noah had an ark and that Daniel was thrown to the lions. It's one of the most popular Bible stories to recount to our children (or, in my case, grandchildren).

But this is absolutely not a nice story for children. It is the story of an innocent man, pushing 80 years of age, who is condemned to death in a most gruesome manner because he chooses loyalty to God over obedience to the state.

And this is absolutely not a moralistic story. How easy it is to make Daniel the hero of the story and to assume that the main point of the text is his example to us, as though what Daniel wants us to go away and think is, "I can dare to be a Daniel." No—the hero is God, the main point of the text is his character and his posture towards us, and what Daniel wanted us to go away thinking is, "I will keep trusting the God whom Daniel knew." As we'll see, Daniel 6 challenges us to serve well and stand firm—but we cannot take a shortcut to that. We will never do these things if we do not know and rely on the truths about God that Daniel did.

SERVE YOUR CITY

In Daniel 1, Daniel and his companions were young men. By the time of this famous passage, Daniel is an old man—his friends may well have died. By this point Daniel's accent would have been the same as that of everybody else around him. His family wouldn't have been picked out in the crowd; they were part of it all.

And Daniel's commitment to the good of the state wasn't in question. He had been a strategic member of successive governments, he had achieved high office under King Nebuchadnezzar, and now King Darius had made him one of the "three high officials ... to whom [the] satraps should give account ... this Daniel became distinguished above all the other high officials and satraps" (6 v 2-3). Presumably, the questions the Jewish exiles had to ask themselves were, "How do we relate to this Babylonian government? Should we be involved in it at all? Should we seek to serve these pagans? Should we wrestle with the complexities of serving a state that stands opposed in almost every way to our own worldview?" Daniel was answering yes to those questions. He did not (as we will see) worship the state, nor did he give unquestioning loyalty to its head, but neither did he withdraw from it. There was for Daniel no circling of the wagons or hiding off with other Jews. Daniel embodied obedience to God's command through the prophet Jeremiah to "seek the welfare of the city where I have sent you into exile, and pray to the LORD on its behalf" (Jeremiah 29 v 7).

Our Western nations may be increasingly committed to a non-Christian worldview and ethical approach. They may be more and more antagonistic to those who wish to live out the law of God. But we are not further from "Jerusalem" than Babylon was. If Daniel could find a way to serve well in exile—to seek the common good, to obey the state wherever he could, to give his time and talents to seeing Babylon flourish—then we can serve well, too. In order not to compromise and blend in with post-Christian culture, we will be tempted to make a run for it, to circle the wagons and isolate ourselves, or to stand outside of our culture and shout at it. Instead, we are to serve, and serve well.

OLD AND YOUNG

The late Eugene Peterson called the life of discipleship "a long obedience in the same direction." Daniel embodies this, too. As a young man, he had drawn his line over the king's diet and refused to cross it. And now his greatest test of all comes toward the end of his life. Most of us, I think, have got the idea that all the temptation comes at the front end of life, when we are young—and if we can just live long enough and keep our faith intact, then we'll reach the point when there's nothing left to tempt us. I don't know about you, but that hasn't worked for me! Perhaps the temptations change and the idols are a different shape, but old age is no defense against facing difficult and costly decisions, nor is it an excuse not to obey.

So for those of us who are older, Daniel 6 stands as an encouragement to us to keep running the race all the way through the tape, and not to let ourselves drift as we approach the end. Equally, if you're younger, don't miss the fact that the decision Daniel made in chapter 1 leads directly to the decision we will see him make in chapter 6. In general (and notwithstanding the power of the Holy Spirit to work in us what we ourselves cannot) what we are in our early years we will be in our later years. If you think you're going to be something at 80 that you're not now, then you'd better start playing catch up. Don't assume that you can be half-hearted now and then somehow make a big push later on. Resolve now to be the kind of man or woman who pleases God, and set your life on that trajectory today, so that you may then prove in the "Chapter 6" stage of your life the benefits of the decisions you made back in your "Chapter 1."

Daniel served well: so well that he was given an exalted position in order to ensure that "the king might suffer no loss"—in other words, to make sure that Darius didn't lose any taxation due to him or territory that belonged to him. And now "the king planned to set him over the whole kingdom" (v 3): to make him his prime minister, or chief of staff. Joyce Baldwin, in her commentary on Daniel, points out that "a senior person known to be impervious to corruption would be an obvious candidate for the top job" (*Daniel*, page 128). And that's the kind of man Daniel was: "impervious to corruption." Again, he was a walking embodiment of the call of the prophets: "[God] has told you, O man, what is good; and what does the LORD require of you but to do justice, and to love kindness?" (Micah 6 v 8).

That's what we're called to be too, as servants of the Lord God. You should not have to walk around your office with a large study Bible tucked under your arm for people to know that you are a follower of the Lord Jesus. You should not need a bunch of bumper stickers declaring your allegiance to Christ. What is far more compelling is to be faithful, to be trustworthy, and to be reliable—to show up when you say you'll show up, to do a full day's job, to finish at the right time, to not steal the pencils or massage the expenses claims, to help your colleagues even when the help is below your pay-grade, to write thank-you notes, to be courteous. It's good to be good at your job. It's a significant thing to be a man of purity in a dirty world, or to be a woman of integrity in a shady world. We are called to do far more than to be good workers and to serve our society well; but we are certainly not called to do less.

Even if it gets us into trouble—as it did Daniel.

KING OR GOD?

Because Daniel is in line for promotion, plenty of other powerful people are not. So this distinguished, diligent servant is also despised. His rivals go and speak to the king. They don't point to Daniel's years of service and to his exemplary character. No: they call him "Daniel, who is one of the exiles from Judah..." (v 13). They are demeaning him and they are questioning his loyalty. Unable to fault him in his work, they have come up with a plan that will force

Daniel to choose between the law of his God and the law of the land. They convince the king to make an irreversible law stating that "whoever makes petition to any god or man for thirty days, except to you, O king, shall be cast into the den of lions" (Daniel 6 v 7).

Something remarkable is happening here: all these ambitious politicians are agreeing! "They came by agreement" before they entered the king's presence (v 6). They may disagree on everything else—politicians have tended to do so through the ages, as well as in our own day—but they agree on their opposition to the living God. They are prepared to plot and scheme and cheat and lie (they claim "all the high officials" are gathered there before the king—but Daniel isn't!) They do not want Daniel and his godliness near them or above them. It was the same when the elites of Jesus' day decided to execute him: "Herod and Pilate became friends with each other that very day, for before this they had been at enmity with each other" (Luke 23 v 12). This is Psalm 2 being enacted on the pages of history:

> "*The kings of the earth set themselves,*
> *and the rulers take counsel together,*
> *against the LORD and against his Anointed [or*
> *in Daniel's case, his servant], saying,*
> *'Let us burst their bonds apart*
> *and cast away their cords from us.'" (v 2-3)*

And so now Daniel must choose: loyalty to the king—and maintain his position, his riches, his reputation, his life—or loyalty to his God—and face death.

You and I have brothers and sisters round the world who today are facing the same choice. I have a friend who's an ophthalmologist (eye doctor, to me and you) who has established an eye clinic in Afghanistan, and I remember several years ago he told me that the only way to identify another believer in public was by a handshake. The way you communicated that you were a believer was to come alongside someone in a crowd and hold their hand in a particular way.

I said, very naively, "What a strange thing to do. Why wouldn't you just tell them you love Jesus?"

"No," he said. "You'd die for doing that."

And, in the last decade, despite their care not to unnecessarily expose themselves to the reach of the state, many have.

We in the West are not in that kind of situation, but we are also a long way from acting as a moral majority (if indeed we ever were more moral, or in a majority). No—we are now a rabble minority, and we need to get used to it, and get used to the challenges and choices that come with that. And you are going to have a really hard time with the rest of Daniel 6 (and the rest of this chapter) if your view of what it means to live for Jesus is primarily about your self-fulfillment, freedom from pain, pursuit of prosperity, and enjoyment of comfort. That superficial contemporary Western view of Christianity will not survive contact with Daniel 6 (or part of the book of Daniel), because Daniel is about choose to die. And that confronts us with the questic that our Afghan brothers and sisters have already an swered: *Is there anything that I would die for?*

THE PRAYER CHALLENGE

Daniel had lived through the events of chapters 1, 2, and 5, and had no doubt heard of the events of Daniel 3. So it should not surprise us to see what he did in response to the edict that banned praying to anyone other than King Darius:

> *"When Daniel knew that the document had been signed, he went to his house where he had windows in his upper chamber open towards Jerusalem. He got down on his knees three times a day and prayed and gave thanks before his God, as he had done previously." (6 v 10)*

Daniel is not simply asserting his right to pray to his own God but protesting against a view of the state that refuses to recognize that there is a law higher than itself. Now as then, governments are capable of making arbitrary laws that refuse to recognize that they are themselves under the jurisdiction of a greater Lawgiver. This is the idea of "natural law," which states that there is built into the very fabric of humanity some natural laws which are inalienable and unchangeable because they were given by the Creator, the ultimate and supreme Lawgiver. No council or majority can (or ought to try to) overturn them. And Daniel is saying here that though he will obey every law King Darius may pass that does not seek to overturn those God-given natural laws, he will not acquiesce in the state making itself supreme.

But more than that, he is demonstrating that his loyalty to his God trumps his loyalty to his earthly king. "What does the LORD require of you but to do justice, and to love kindness, *and to walk humbly with your God?*" (Micah 6 v 8, my emphasis). Daniel has served well; but now he will stand firm.

Was he tempted to compromise? He could have said to himself, *What is 30 days out of an entire lifetime? I've prayed a lot in my life—I'm sure the Lord would understand if I just skipped prayer for a month.* Or, *It doesn't really matter where you pray, so I'll change the location and timing of my prayers (and close the windows), and then nobody will know I'm doing it.* But he doesn't: "He got down on his knees three times a day and prayed and gave thanks before his God, *as he had done previously*" (Daniel 6 v 10, my emphasis). He changed nothing.

That little phrase "as he had done previously" is striking. If Daniel's prayer life had been spasmodic—if it had ebbed and flowed depending on how he felt—his colleagues could never have counted on catching him. It was the very regularity and faithfulness of Daniel's praying that made it possible for them to catch him in the act. Again we are seeing that a time of crisis in life reveals the truth about us; it does not create it. To mix metaphors, when the tide of opposition rises high, we see what is really behind the walls of our homes and hearts.

So here is a very challenging question: would it make any substantial difference in our lives—individually or as churches—if prayer were to be banned for the next thirty days? What possibility would there be of the authorities coming to your home, or your church, and catching you at prayer? Would anyone be able to say to them, "Ah, yes, Alistair prays every day, at this time, without fail"?

Speaking for a moment specifically about the American context, isn't there something wrong with us as a church that we have expended such effort on the absence of prayer in our state-run public schools while being unprepared to acknowledge the absence of prayer in our local churches or to increase our own commitment to praying? It's almost like a smokescreen. If I can make a fuss about the lack of prayer over there, then maybe I can forget about the lack of prayer in my own life or in my own church. Daniel's challenge is an unavoidable one. He still prayed. He just did what he had always done. Is that what you have always done? Will it be?

Daniel didn't let his enemies down. When they went to his house to spy on him, there he was, praying just as he always did. This is not a case of Daniel making a public display of devotion (in Babylonian houses, windows were small and high up on the walls); it's a case of the plotters making an intrusion into his personal affairs. And Daniel had made his choice—loyalty to God and death if necessary.

And so his enemies point out to the king, "Daniel ... pays no attention to you, O king, or the injunction you have signed, but makes his petition three times a day" (v 13). The implication is that he regards his commitment to God of such importance that obedience to this manmade edict is totally unacceptable. As loyal as he was to the duties of the empire, nobody could be in any doubt in Daniel's case about his allegiance to the kingdom of God. And so, the king having been reminded by the plotters that his edict was irreversible, Daniel was "brought and cast into the den of lions" (v 16)—to his death—"and a stone was brought and laid on the mouth of the den" (v 17). As Sinclair Ferguson puts it, "This was the hand of the kingdom of darkness seeking to annihilate the kingdom of God" (*Daniel*, page 138).

TWO EMPTY TOMBS

As every child knows, the lions' den was not the death of Daniel. The next morning the king, after a sleepless night, rushes down to the den and calls, "O Daniel … has your God, whom you serve continually, been able to deliver you from the lions?" (v 20). And a voice answers. "O king, live forever! My God sent his angel and shut the lion's mouths, and they have not harmed me, because I was blameless before him; and also before you, O king, I have done no harm" (v 21-22). Daniel was innocent of failing to obey God in this matter of prayer; and he was innocent of any actual harm to Darius. "So Daniel was taken up out of the den" (v 23), emerging alive from the place that should have been his tomb.

At this moment our thoughts should be thrown forwards down the centuries to another early morning, and another place of death sealed by a stone rolled over its entrance, and another voice of a man who was innocent of the charges against him and who was innocent of failing to obey God in any matter at all:

> *Vainly they watch his bed,*
> *Jesus my Savior,*
> *Vainly they seal the dead,*
> *Jesus my Lord!*
> *Up from the grave he arose …*

Death cannot keep his prey,
Jesus my Savior,
He tore the bars away,
Jesus my Lord!

Sinclair Ferguson points out that in the Old Testament, the destructive power of lions is a metaphor for the chaos and disharmony of this fallen world. It's no surprise, therefore, that Peter chooses to describe Satan as a "roaring lion" who looks to "devour" believers by dragging them from their faith (1 Peter 5 v 8). And it is wonderful to read Isaiah's description of the promised kingdom to come, where the lion will lie down with the calf (Isaiah 11 v 6). In Daniel's den, we get a glimpse of the coming kingdom, where lions whose only object is to destroy and consume are transformed into placid, peaceful creatures.

This den becomes a place of deliverance for Daniel, just as Jesus' tomb is a place of deliverance—and, gloriously, deliverance not only for him but for all who trust in him. The cross and tomb are where we are invited into the kingdom, and where chaos begins to be transformed into peace.

But in the place of deliverance, there is also destruction: "The king commanded, and those men who had maliciously accused Daniel were brought and cast into the den of lions—they, their children, and their wives" (Daniel 6 v 24)—and there was no angel to deliver them.

This is a somber note in the story, and it is worth pointing out that this punishment was one of Persian law, not of God's. It was the king's command, not the

Lord's. But the punishment that fell on them is also a glimpse of the divine punishment that will one day fall on those who have spent their lives opposing the kingdom of God and fighting its King. God delivers his people and destroys his enemies. He did it in the flood, rescuing Noah from his judgment. He did it at the Red Sea, giving his people a dry path to walk along before the waters returned to drown the pursuing Egyptian army. He did it at the lions' den. And he will do it one day to come, when Jesus finally returns and the kingdom comes in all its fullness, and the lion lies down with the calf and God restores his people and judges his enemies. What you do with the one who hung on the cross and walked out of the tomb decides what God will do with you for eternity.

A HIGHER THRONE

Don't doubt that there are going to be moments when you face the same choice that Daniel did: between loyalty to the prevailing winds of our culture and maintaining your position, riches, reputation, and perhaps even life—and loyalty to God, at great and increasing cost. Don't look back over your shoulder and pine for the supposed good old days. Don't look forward with a sense of dread. Don't run away and try to remove yourself and your family from a pagan culture. Remember to lift your eyes to a higher throne, a greater King, and a nobler cause—and you will be equipped to serve well in every way you can, and to stand firm when you must. The empty tomb reminds us of the kind of God whom we serve: one who is worthy of our praise, and who has delivered and will deliver us, and around whose throne one day we will stand with Daniel and sing—not of ourselves, nor of Daniel, but of him.

TAKE HEART – GOD WINS

What do you expect life is going to be like for you and for your church? How well are things going right now, and how well are they going to go in the future?

Some of us are natural optimists. Our general approach is that things will likely work out fine. We like sermons and books that emphasize the victory of God and his church. To this view, Daniel 7 says it's going to work out even better than we thought.

Some of us are natural pessimists. Given the way Western culture is turning against Christianity and given the pandemic and its effects that we are living through, it feels to me that more and more of us are pessimistic. We prefer sermons and books that equip the saints to walk through the suffering and rejection that we know is part of the Christian life. Daniel 7 says that if we think everything is not going to work out well at all, we're not wrong—but there is more hope than we realize.

Daniel 7 moors us spiritually, and emotionally, in something beyond our optimism or our pessimism. It tells us that things are far worse than we thought, and far better than we've ever hoped.

And it does so by bringing us a completely different way of looking at history, the world, and eternity. Welcome to "apocalyptic" writing.

ENTER THE VIDEO GAME

Apocalyptic writing is literary shock treatment—a genre to be used in an emergency. It is employed in the Bible, including in the second half of the book of Daniel, when the drama is so perplexing and so overwhelming that what needs to be said cannot be encapsulated by the normal mechanisms of addressing or describing life. God employs apocalyptic language in order to express that which falls outside the normal boundaries of our use of language.

Theological scholars have debated just about everything that is said in the second half of Daniel. Many Christians reach chapter 7 and turn into theological Sherlock Holmeses, acting like sleuths who are going to uncover secret, hidden mysteries about which to sound clever in front of Christian friends. (It won't work—watch their eyes glaze over.) But the second half of the book of Daniel, beginning in chapter 7, is not included in the Bible just so that we can argue about exact timings and enjoy trying to work out what each image corresponds to in history, but never actually derive anything helpful for real life from it. No—the point of these chapters is to make clear that, contrary to appearances, God is on the throne and the future is securely in his hands.

You might think, *That's what the first six chapters were about, weren't they?* Exactly! Remember, the purpose of the book of Daniel is to say again and again essentially the same thing: that God is in charge of the whole universe and you can trust him. So that is what the second six chapters of the book are about too; it is the perspective that changes. This truth is no longer being told in terms of the unfolding historical drama of the experience of those who lived in exile—it is now being described in a very different, amazing, dimension.

The way to understand these verses is to picture them. Some of us find that harder than others. If you live in a world of video games, you'll find this much easier than if you live in a world of books. Gamers are finely attuned to seeing something visually and then making deductions from what they see—and Daniel 7 is like one big, unfolding, rapidly-moving video game. But regardless of whether you are naturally a gamer or a reader, Daniel 7 is not straightforward. As the theologian and historian Chad Van Dixhoorn puts it, mapping the high points of the Bible is tiring work. But it will be worth it. Daniel 7 opens with him shifting to the first person and saying, "I saw in my vision by night, and behold..." (v 2); he's asking us to look—to watch.

So here is the first part of the chapter:

> "Behold, the four winds of heaven were stirring up the great sea. And four great beasts came up out of the sea, different from one another. The first was like a lion and had eagles' wings. Then as I looked its wings were plucked off, and it was lifted up from the ground and made to stand on two feet like a man, and the mind of a man was given to

it. And behold, another beast, a second one, like a bear. It was raised up on one side. It had three ribs in its mouth between its teeth; and it was told, 'Arise, devour much flesh.' After this I looked, and behold, another, like a leopard, with four wings of a bird on its back. And the beast had four heads, and dominion was given to it. After this I saw in the night visions, and behold, a fourth beast, terrifying and dreadful and exceedingly strong. It had great iron teeth; it devoured and broke in pieces and stamped what was left with its feet. It was different from all the beasts that were before it, and it had ten horns. I considered the horns, and behold, there came up among them another horn, a little one, before which three of the first horns were plucked up by the roots. And behold, in this horn were eyes like the eyes of a man, and a mouth speaking great things." (v 2-8)

So what are we seeing?

FOUR EMPIRES AND A TERRIFYING MAN

The four beasts Daniel sees each rise from the stirred-up sea (v 2-3). In the Bible, sea often represents the chaos of a sinful world (for example, Isaiah 57 v 20 and Psalm 68 v 21-22); likewise, the Babylonians thought of the sea as a monstrous place, and their myths told of monsters that came up out of it. Now the wind blows from heaven, and as a result these beasts emerge—terrible and powerful, as we shall see, but nevertheless not outside the control of heaven.

Because we've already read Daniel 2, we can safely assume (I think!) that we're dealing here with the same empires as there. Further, just like today, back then nations often represented themselves with an animal. So today Scotland uses the rampant lion, Russia the bear, and the USA the eagle. (If you're American, be thankful that Benjamin Franklin did not get his way—he suggested a turkey!) And in Daniel's vision we therefore see:

- A lion with eagles' wings. This represents Nebuchadnezzar and Babylon. Babylon had this as a symbol on many of its gates, so Daniel must have been familiar with this simply from living in the city.
- A bear: the Medo-Persian Empire. This bear was likely "raised up on one side" because one side of the Medo-Persian Empire was stronger than the other. This is not a teddy bear. It is a scary brute with three ribs in its mouth. The point here is probably straightforward: it had a voracious appetite. It devoured people.
- A leopard—swift and dangerous—with wings to further speed its progress and four heads so that it could look in different directions simultaneously. What kind of empire is being described here? Again, it matches the history of the empire of Alexander the Great. He moved with unmatched speed to destroy the Medo-Persian Empire. With 30,000 troops he took on the power of the Medo-Persian Empire in a number of battles in which he was opposed by between 150,000 and 800,000 soldiers. And he

won them all, so that by the age of 32 he controlled Greece, Egypt, Persia, and further east to the borders of India. Notice here that Daniel says that "dominion was given to [the third beast]" (v 6). In the history books it seems as though Alexander seized his power. *No*, says Daniel. *His power was given—given by God.* How do we explain this empire? Dominion was given to it. How about, much later, the British Empire? Dominion was given to it—and taken from it. The rise of the Soviet Empire, of the United States, of, yes, even North Korea? Dominion was given to each of them. These kingdoms are not accidents or a diversion from the divine plan.

• The fourth beast is confusing because there is no point of resemblance to any creature on earth. It's as though this state is so terrifying and dreadful that no creature or combination of creatures can begin to describe its nature. It had iron teeth, it devoured, it broke in pieces, and it stamped upon what was left with its feet; it was different from all the beasts that were before it. And the brutality and the terrifying nature of the advance of Rome is recorded here in this visionary picture. The horns denote power—most animals have two, but this one has ten. Don't try to match them to Roman kings or European nations or whatever else. They simply mean that this empire was really, really powerful.

And then the vision focuses on a little horn. It seems to grow more powerful than any of the other horns. It looks as though it is essentially evil personified. It has human eyes and a mouth—it seems to represent an individual (or a type of individual): very possibly, the person (or people) to whom Paul is referring in 2 Thessalonians 2 when he describes the "man of lawlessness." There, he is speaking to a church facing increasing persecution from the might of the Roman Empire and wondering when Jesus will come back (or if he already has) and what is going to happen to them as his people. And Paul says:

> "For that day [of Christ's return] will not come, unless the rebellion comes first, and the man of lawlessness is revealed, the son of destruction, who opposes and exalts himself against every so-called god or object of worship, so that he takes his seat in the temple of God, proclaiming himself to be God. Do you not remember that when I was still with you I told you these things? And you know what is restraining him now so that he may be revealed in his time. For the mystery of lawlessness is already at work. Only he who now restrains it will do so until he is out of the way. And then the lawless one will be revealed, whom the Lord Jesus will kill with the breath of his mouth and bring to nothing by the appearance of his coming. The coming of the lawless one is by the activity of Satan with all power and false signs and wonders, and with all wicked deception for those who are perishing, because they refused to love the truth and so be saved." (v 3-10)

This helps us to make sense of Daniel's "little horn." He is, it seems, the "man of lawlessness," who represents proud, blasphemous humanity in its rebellion against God. And, while those who oppose God and his law deliberately and aggressively are ultimately under the control of the sovereign God, their coming is "by the activity of Satan" (Daniel 7 v 9). In other words, it's not possible for us to understand Daniel 7 (or, indeed, the whole of the Bible) without recognizing that there is a devil, and that he is active and hostile.

The great Welsh preacher Martyn Lloyd-Jones said once in an interview a few decades ago, "I am certain that one of the main causes of the ill-state of the church today lies in the fact that the devil is being forgotten" (*The Christian Warfare*, page 292). The saints of God throughout history and in our world right now have suffered and are suffering at the hands of evil people who are, mostly without realizing it, being directed by the evil one. The people of this world are being deceived and wooed by worldviews and religions that have been dreamed up by the evil one. The difficulty that many of us have in dealing with these kinds of ideas is because of the fact that we pay scant attention to the devil. The Scriptures never give us leave to make that mistake.

What are we to make of all this? We are not to be surprised when we find Christianity maligned and marginalized, when we hear of Christians being prosecuted and persecuted, or when we find ourselves being told we are extremists, haters, and bigots. For a few hundred years in the West we have been able to kid ourselves that the normal experience of God's people is to be considered respectable and honorable, to be able to voice our views in the public square and be welcomed, and to be able to speak to those in power and be listened to. It was not ever thus, and it is no longer thus. We are back to the normal experience of the church: facing opposition and being called to stand firm and undergo suffering for our faith.

So where is God in all this? Daniel is about to see...

GOD ARRIVES

"As I looked,
thrones were placed,
*   and the Ancient of Days took his seat;*
his clothing was white as snow,
*   and the hair of his head like pure wool;*
his throne was fiery flames;
*   its wheels were burning fire.*
A stream of fire issued
*   and came out from before him;*
a thousand thousands served him,
*   and ten thousand times ten thousand stood before*
him;
the court sat in judgment,
*   and the books were opened.*

"I looked then because of the sound of the great
words that the horn was speaking. And as I looked,
the beast was killed, and its body destroyed and
given over to be burned with fire. As for the rest
of the beasts, their dominion was taken away, but
their lives were prolonged for a season and a time."
(v 9-12)

The Ancient of Days is a description of God. Him being seated on his throne reminds us that he holds the position of ultimate authority; his clothing and his hair are representative of his purity; his fiery throne and the fire issuing from him indicate the reality of his judgment; and the fact that there are thousands upon thousands who serve him points to the magnitude of what's going on. So here is a picture of the purity and the power and the judgment of God, in images used elsewhere in the Bible (see Exodus 3 and 19, and Ezekiel 1).

What is Daniel being shown here? First, that he is not alone. He may be plowing a lonely furrow of godliness in the heart of the Babylonian Empire at this point, but in serving the Ancient of Days he takes his place with ten thousand times ten thousand, if only he has eyes to see it. Second, that the kingdoms of man start to crumble as the court sits in judgment.

All of the injustice and all of the hatred will one day face a reckoning when the books are opened. While the views and influences represented by those ancient God-opposing kingdoms are still with us—their "lives were prolonged"—all fell, and all will fall. Kingdoms and philosophies opposed to God may linger, but they will not last.

And then another figure enters our scene…

NO ORDINARY HUMAN

> "I saw in the night visions,
> and behold, with the clouds of heaven
> there came one like a son of man,
> and he came to the Ancient of Days

and was presented before him.
And to him was given dominion
    and glory and a kingdom,
that all peoples, nations, and languages
    should serve him;
his dominion is an everlasting dominion,
    which shall not pass away,
and his kingdom one
    that shall not be destroyed.

"As for me, Daniel, my spirit within me was
anxious, and the visions of my head alarmed me. I
approached one of those who stood there and asked
him the truth concerning all this. So he told me and
made known to me the interpretation of the things.
'These four great beasts are four kings who shall
arise out of the earth. But the saints of the Most
High shall receive the kingdom and possess the
kingdom forever, forever and ever.'"

(Daniel 7 v 13-18)

Here is Jesus. He is "one like a son of man"—a human. But he is not any ordinary human! He is coming to the Ancient of Days to be given a kingdom in which "all people, nations, and languages should serve him" and his rule "shall not pass away."

Notice what Jesus is doing in this scene: he is coming to the Ancient of Days. He is not coming *from* the Ancient of Days. So this is surely a description not of Jesus coming from heaven at the end of time, but rather a description of Jesus going back to heaven after his death, resurrection, and ascension. This is his coronation.

Reading this in the twenty-first century after Jesus returned to heaven, we are not reading Daniel 7 v 13-14 as a vision of something that will happen but as a vision of something that has already happened.

In Acts 1, "as [the disciples] were looking on, [Jesus] was lifted up, and a cloud took him out of their sight" (v 9), and Daniel 7 v 13-14 is what happened next, behind that cloud as it were. When Jesus told his disciples shortly before his ascension that "all authority in heaven and on earth has been given to me," this is the rule he was speaking of (Matthew 28 v 18).

This reality is why we are to "go ... and make disciples of all nations, baptizing them in the name of the Father and of the Son and of the Holy Spirit" (v 19). The work of proclaiming the gospel throughout the world is a logical deduction from the truth about who Christ is and what Christ has accomplished and where Christ is right now. Increasingly, the cultural view of mission (whether it's down your street or across the seas) is that it involves evangelicals going out to foist upon people something that is unhelpful to and unnecessary for them. Respect and love requires, the argument goes, that we leave nice Muslim people, nice Hindu people, nice atheist and agnostic and spiritual people alone to get on with living the way that seems right and feels best to them. How intolerant and arrogant for us to try to compel others to look at things our way! Well, if Jesus is not the son of man whom Daniel saw in his vision, then yes, evangelism is the worst thing we could do. But if Jesus is that son of man, then there is coming a day when every knee will bow to him, and some will shout with joy but others will wail with anguish—and how can we be silent about that and still call ourselves loving of others?

GOD HAS WON, BUT THE WAR ISN'T OVER

Daniel 7 is not easy (I did warn you), and we've only reached just over the halfway point! Through the rest of the chapter, Daniel requests and receives further details to help him understand the vision. But by this point, the headline is clear:

> *God has won, and God will win, and his people will reign—but the war is not over yet.*

So that little horn will make "war with the saints and [prevail] over them" (Daniel 7 v 21)—but one day, the Ancient of Days will come and "judgment [will be] given for the saints of the Most High, and the time [will come] when the saints [possess] the kingdom" (v 22).

The story is not that this great triumph has taken place and that therefore for the balance of time until Christ returns the people of God are just going to be able to enjoy themselves and relax and have a nice time while they wait. No, we are in the era of now-but-not-yet: we are living in the period of time between the coronation of Christ and the final glorious victory of Christ. We're in the midst of what the Westminster Confession refers to as "a continual and irreconcilable war." It is a war that will be won, because it has already been won—but the fight continues. As Don Carson puts it, in our day "the gospel is boldly advancing under the contested reign and inevitable victory of King

Jesus" (thegospelcoalition.org/conference_media/what-is-the-gospel/, accessed 7/23/20).

That may feel terrifying. It felt that way for Daniel: "As for me, Daniel, my spirit within me was anxious, and the visions of my head alarmed me" (v 15). Even by the end of the chapter, once he's received a little more by way of explanation, he concludes, "As for me, Daniel, my thoughts greatly alarmed me, and my color changed" (v 28). What alarmed him so much? Presumably it was gaining this insight into the fact that, though the end was certain, the path to reach it would continue to be harder than he had imagined, despite God's people already having experienced invasion, defeat, devastation, exile, and danger.

We need this perspective too. This life will not be easy, because there is raging around us "a continual and irreconcilable war," and neutrality is not an option. Life may get harder. Society may get unfriendlier. Faith in Christ may become still more unacceptable and obedience to Christ still more costly. But the recurring theme of Daniel 7 is that the saints of God will receive the kingdom and possess it forever and ever. Jesus reigns, and Jesus will return. We may not understand every part of the picture that Daniel paints in chapter 7, but stand back and see the broad sweep of it. God has won. God wins. And so we will prevail too, beyond the battle that you and I are a part of and must fight well in. When we see the drama that unfolds here in Daniel 7, and see our part in it, our view of our world, and our lives, and our eternity is altered entirely.

"In the world you will have tribulation," the Son of Man told his subjects in the days before his coronation (John 16 v 33). "But take heart; I have overcome the world."

EPILOGUE:
JESUS SHALL REIGN

A missionary was returning to the United States, back in the days when overseas travel was only by ship. It happened that this missionary was on the same ship as an acclaimed national figure, and as the boat docked in New York, there were huge numbers of people gathered on the quay to greet this popular man with banners and signs. The photographers were lined up to take pictures of his return for all the newspapers.

As the missionary scanned the faces on the quay, he realized that no one had come to welcome him. He had been gone for years, laboring in the cause of Christ, and no one had turned up to greet him.

As he began to submerge in waves of self-pity, a truth struck him as clearly as if a voice had spoken it to him from heaven (which, in a sense, it had):

"Do not be discouraged. You have not reached home. This isn't it."

This is the message of Daniel. *Do not be discouraged. You have not reached home. This isn't it.* You will find no self-pity, retreat, or compromise in any of its chapters. Daniel and his friends were pushed hard. They found themselves falling—literally, into the furnace and the lions' den. But Psalm 118 v 13-14 was true for them, as it is true for us:

> *"I was pushed hard, so that I was falling,*
> *but the LORD helped me.*
> *The LORD is my strength and my song;*
> *he has become my salvation."*

We know, and will know increasingly, what it means to be pushed hard by the antagonism of our culture. We know, and will know increasingly, what it is like to feel that we cannot stand. But we can also know the help of the Lord, who is sovereign. We can know what it is to be strengthened to hold the line, to obey, to witness, and to act with compassion. We can keep singing of the Lord who has saved us—who has saved us not from trials but through trials, and who supremely has saved us from his judgment so that we may look forward to reaching home beyond our death.

Pushed hard, falling, helped, strengthened, singing, saved. By faith, that was the story of the exiles in Babylon, a long way from Jerusalem; and by faith, it is the story of exiles in this world today, a long way from heaven but walking always towards it.

What will we sing as we journey on? We could do worse than sing what the Scotsman Eric Liddell sang as he headed off to China, for it is a song that encapsulates much of the truth about God that Daniel 1 – 7 sets before us. Eric Liddell was a Scotsman who played rugby for Scotland and won gold in the 1924 Olympics in the 400 meters. He had been due to race in the 200 meters, for which he was the favorite, but the race fell on a Sunday, and his conscience did not permit him to race on Sundays. He had drawn his line and refused to cross it despite significant pressure being put on him to do so.

Nevertheless, as a gold medalist and rugby international Liddell was something of a hero. And then he decided to leave Edinburgh for China to work there as a missionary. When he left Waverley station, crowds flocked to see him off, many of them youngsters intrigued to see this amazing athlete who was giving everything up and leaving everything behind to go to China to teach children about Jesus.

Liddell could have been a double gold medalist if he had just compromised a little, just once. He could have enjoyed a comfortable, prosperous, and popular life in Scotland. What a strange, nonsensical way it was that he chose to live his life! Unless, of course, you believe that the kingdoms of this world will give way to the kingdom of Jesus Christ, and that this is not your home.

Liddell believed that, and so he lived that. As he boarded the train, he let down the window in his carriage, silenced the crowd, and shouted out, "Christ for the world. For the world needs Christ." That was his parting shot. And then he led them in the singing of this hymn:

Jesus shall reign where'er the sun
Doth his successive journeys run;
His kingdom stretch from shore to shore,
Till moons shall wax and wane no more.

If by God's grace you understand that Jesus reigns, then you will live like Eric Liddell, even when it seems that the world is triumphing and that Christ's church is under pressure. That does not necessarily mean that you will go to China; but it does mean that because you have faith in the God who rules, you will live bravely, live confidently, and live obeying Jesus and proclaiming Jesus, even in a land that neither understands your decisions nor welcomes your message.

Don't look back to the "glory days." Live well in this day. If you're a banker, be a banker to the glory of God. If you're a teacher, teach to the glory of God. If you're a scientist, research to the glory of God. If you're a salesman, sell to the glory of God. Just be who you are, where you are, obedient and confident in the conviction that God is accomplishing the eternal counsel of his will and that he's drawn you into the story into which he drew Daniel and those exiles: the story of how he is bringing his kingdom to this world until the day when it stretches from shore to shore.

Living like that will not be easy. It may well get harder. But it is possible, because when we are pushed hard and we are falling, we have a God who is more than capable of helping us, saving us, and causing us to sing of him. We can be—we must be—brave by faith.

A few years ago, the US Supreme Court decided to change the definition of marriage. They were taking to themselves an authority that belongs only to God. It was one of those moments when Christians in a nation realize that they are not at home in their nation any more. I expect that, wherever you live, there will be more of those moments to come as we are increasingly buffeted, marginalized, and ostracized. I wrote in my journal that evening, "This is the saddest day of my life in America."

And then I added:

> *"But I know that God is still in charge. So we proceed accordingly."*

I know that—and I resolved to do that—because I know the God whom Daniel knew. Do you?

Do not be discouraged. You have not reached home. This isn't it. And Jesus shall reign.

BIBLIOGRAPHY

Joyce Baldwin, *Daniel: An Introduction and Commentary* (IVP UK, 1978)

Sinclair Ferguson, *The Communicator's Commentary: Daniel* (Word Books, 1988)

D. Martyn Lloyd-Jones, *The Christian Warfare* (Banner of Truth, 1976)

Richard Niebuhr, *The Nature and Destiny of Man* (Westminster John Knox Press, 1996)

J.B. Phillips, *Your God Is Too Small* (Touchstone, 2004)

Melanie Phillips, *The World Turned Upside Down* (Encounter Books, 2011)

John Stott, *Authentic Christianity* (Marshalls, 1985)

John Stott, *The Message of Acts* (IVP UK/IVP Academic, 1991)

Rico Tice, *Honest Evangelism* (The Good Book Company, 2015)

BIBLICAL | RELEVANT | ACCESSIBLE

At The Good Book Company, we are dedicated to helping Christians and local churches grow. We believe that God's growth process always starts with hearing clearly what he has said to us through his timeless word—the Bible.

Ever since we opened our doors in 1991, we have been striving to produce Bible-based resources that bring glory to God. We have grown to become an international provider of user-friendly resources to the Christian community, with believers of all backgrounds and denominations using our books, Bible studies, devotionals, evangelistic resources, and DVD-based courses.

We want to equip ordinary Christians to live for Christ day by day, and churches to grow in their knowledge of God, their love for one another, and the effectiveness of their outreach.

Call us for a discussion of your needs or visit one of our local websites for more information on the resources and services we provide.

Your friends at The Good Book Company

thegoodbook.com | thegoodbook.co.uk
thegoodbook.com.au | thegoodbook.co.nz
thegoodbook.co.in